ESSENTIAL SELECTIVE

MATHEMATICAL REASONING

5 Mathematical Reasoning Test Papers

RAY LEE I JIMMY LIU

To Cookie, my light,
and to Phoebe who I hope
can one day figure out all the questions in this book.

Five Senses Education Pty Ltd
2/195 Prospect Highway
Seven Hills 2147
New South Wales Australia

First Published 2023

Lee, Ray and Liu, Jimmy

Essential Selective
Mathematical Reasoning Book 2
ISBN 978-1-76032-534-3

2023 02 17

Contents

Preface

This book is designed to help students prepare for the Selective High School Placement Test. It consists of five mathematical reasoning practice exam papers and is suitable for use by Year 5 and 6 students. The exam papers are designed to the exact format of the Selective High School Placement Test, with hand picked questions that closely relate to past Selective High School Examination questions.

Success in this extremely competitive exam requires commitment and hard work. We hope these practice exam papers can help you achieve your goals.

Five Senses Education

Selective Practice Test

Mathematical Reasoning 6 (Time allowed: 40 min)

INSTRUCTIONS

1. Write your Name on the cover page.
2. There are 35 questions in this paper. For each question there are five possible answers, A, B, C, D and E. Choose the one correct answer and record your choice on the separate answer sheet. If you make a mistake, erase thoroughly and try again.
3. You will not lose marks for incorrect answers, so you should attempt all 35 questions
4. You must complete the answer sheet within the time limit. There will not be any extra time at the end of the exam to record your answers on the answer sheet.
5. You can use the question paper for working out, but no extra paper is allowed.

Name: ______________________________

1 What is the cheapest buy at this fruit store?

A 1kg of watermelons for $5

B $1\frac{1}{2}$ kg of watermelons for $8

C 750g of watermelons for $4

D 500g of watermelons for $3

E 100g of watermelons for $0.60

2 Round off to the nearest thousand before adding the values.

Then, 24690 + 1495 = ?

A 25000

B 26185

C 26000

D 27000

E 21000

3 Step 1 Step 2 Step 3

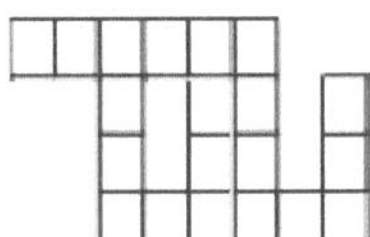

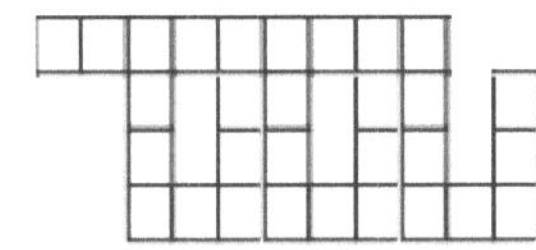

5 cm long 8 cm long 11 cm long

In which step will the figure be 1.58 m long?

A 49

B 50

C 51

D 52

E 53

4 The Mynes Verithia is a plant which can live in a certain difference in temperature, within any temperature range above freezing.

If it can only survive in a temperature difference of 10.45°C, which of the following would the plant survive in?

A -1.00°C → 9.5°C

B 6.65°C → 17.05°C

C 26.54°C → 36.99°C

D 356.35°C → 375.78°C

E -6.00°C → 4.45°C

5 What is the proportion of the shaded area with respect to the large rectangle?

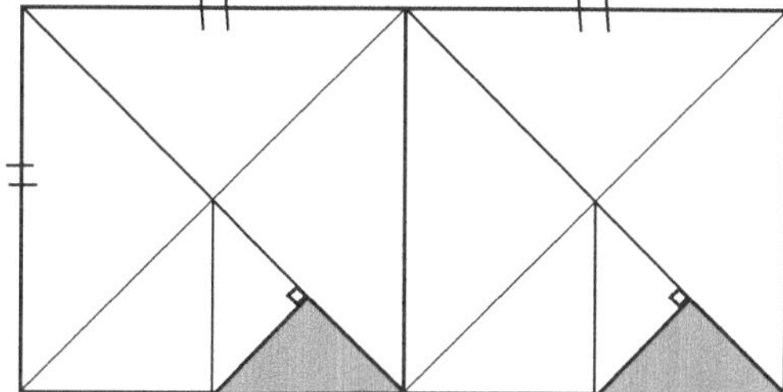

A $\frac{1}{4}$

B $\frac{1}{8}$

C $\frac{1}{12}$

D $\frac{2}{12}$

E $\frac{1}{16}$

6 Mr Huang is 42 and his son John is 17.

How old will Mr Huang be when John is half his father's age?

A 50

B 54

C 58

D 60

E 70

7 Adam is drawing a sector graph.

It will show how the 27 children in his class come to school.

18 of the children are dropped off by their parents.

What angle should Adam use for the sector that shows the students who are dropped off by their parents?

A 180°

B 240°

C 270°

D 90°

E 45°

8 In Blockworld, all the inhabitants have blocks for heads. One particular individual, has a head that looks like this (the L denotes the left-side of his face).

L

Choose the correct statement for when he looks in the mirror:

A the star will be on the left side of his face.

B his whole face will be upside down.

C the diamond will be on the right side of his face.

D the star will be on the right side of his face.

E none of above

9 In the Blue and Violet classes, there are 16 students in class Blue and 24 students in class Violet.

The average mark for a maths test in class Blue was 80% and in class Violet is 90%.

What would be the average mark of two classes?

A 90%
B 86%
C 82%
D 85%
E 80%

10 What will be the volume of the following cube if the middle blocks on each face and the corners of each face are removed?

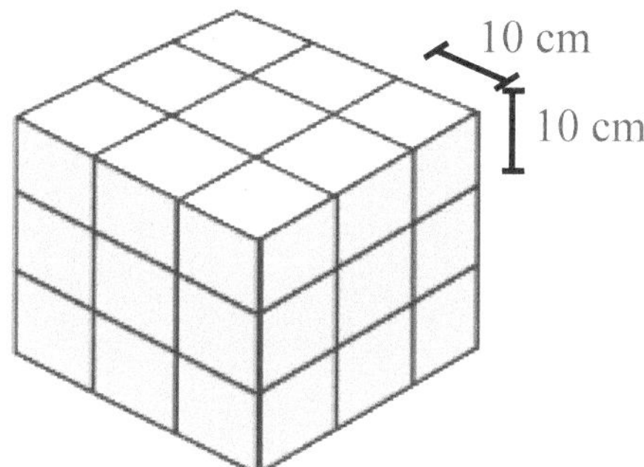

A 12000cm^3
B 13000cm^3
C 14000cm^3
D 15000cm^3
E 16000cm^3

11 In a certain class, all the students specialise in only one sport, either: basketball, badminton, or soccer.

If there is 1 less than 2 times more badminton players than soccer players and 1 less than 2 times more basketball players than badminton players, how many students are in the class if 5 people play only soccer?

A 35

B 34

C 31

D 28

E 24

12 For a certain carpet, every 25 cm^2 there is a picture of a flower.

If my entire house has this carpet, and in total there are 100 m^2, how many flowers will I be able to see on my floor?

A 400

B 4 000

C 40 000

D 400 000

E 4 000 000

13 Andrew started going to the gym. He is able to lift different weights for different exercises.

In total, he lifts 165kg split into 6 different exercises as shown in the graph below.

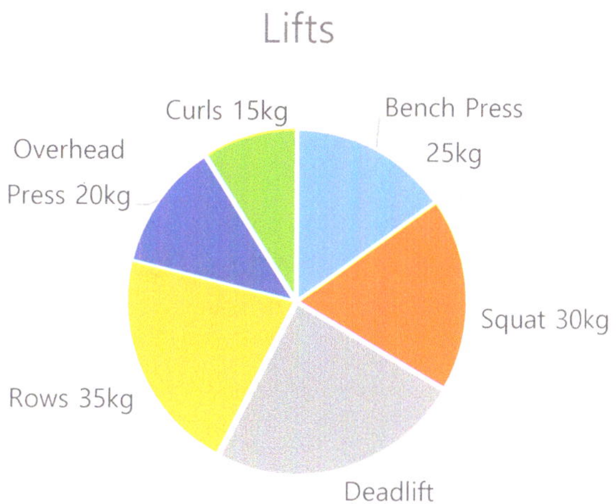

How much did Andrew lift altogether on deadlift, squats and bench press?

A 125 kg
B 115 kg
C 105 kg
D 100 kg
E 95 kg

14 Consider the following decimals.

0.739, 0.076, 0.704, 0.927

What is the sum of the smallest and largest of them?

A 1.003
B 0.815
C 0.780
D 1.631
E 1.424

15 Three consecutive numbers have an average of 74. What is the largest of these numbers?

A 72
B 73
C 74
D 75
E 76

16 The total height of three boys is 500 centimetres. Dennis is 10 centimetres taller than Jeremy who is 20 centimetres taller than Andrew.

What is Andrew's height?

A 140 centimetres
B 145 centimetres
C 150 centimetres
D 155 centimetres
E 160 centimetres

17 Two children shared $900.00 so that the younger child received $\frac{1}{4}$ of the amount received by the older child.

How much did the older child get?

A $800.00
B $750.00
C $700.00
D $680.00
E $720.00

18 To make Castle Hill more beautiful, a large number of flowers were planted.

Due to the lack of rainfall and heat, 8 out of every 20 flowers died.

If 380 flowers dies, how many were planted?

A 1000

B 950

C 500

D 750

E 2000

19 The name of this triangle is

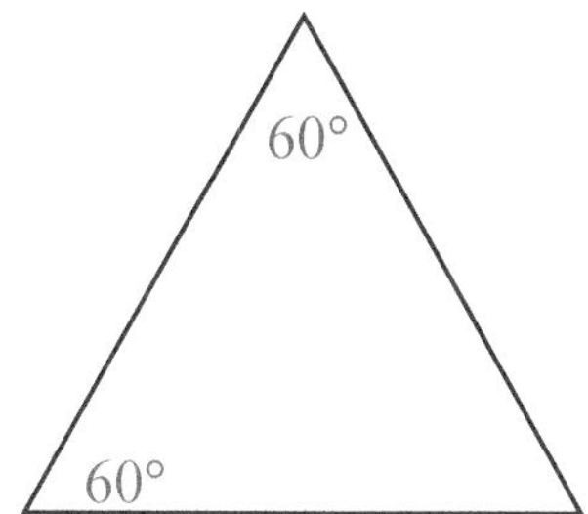

A scalene

B isosceles

C equilateral

D right

E not enough information

20 In a taekwondo club, members are split into three classes: X, Y and Z. There are 200 members of which each of the three classes were allocated with 25%, 25% and 50% students respectively.

In class X and Y, 50% of the members are girls.

However, class Z contains a 1:3 ratio of boys and girls.

How many boys are there in the entire members' base?

A 75

B 72

C 70

D 63

E 60

21 From the temperature graph, what was the greatest range in temperature for a one-hour period?

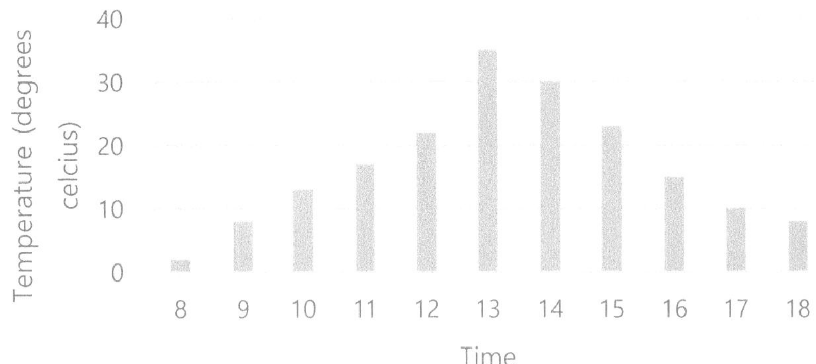

A 10ºC

B 13ºC

C 15ºC

D 17ºC

E 19ºC

22 The following container holds 360ml. Find x.

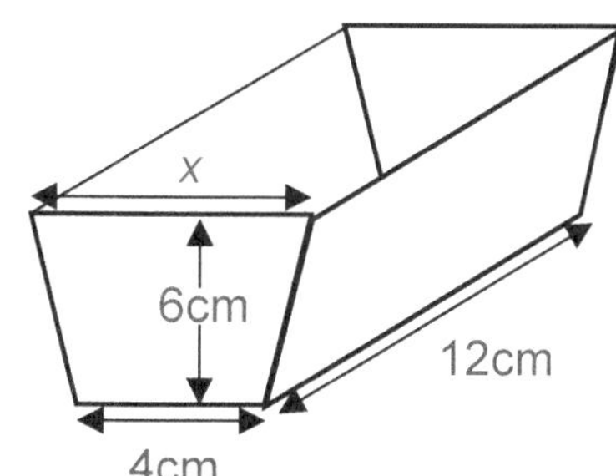

A 4cm

B 5cm

C 6cm

D 7cm

E 8cm

23 What is the smallest number of different colours needed to paint a triangular prism so that no adjacent faces have the same colour?

A 2

B 3

C 4

D 5

E 6

24 Andrew has 20 cards. Dennis has $3\frac{3}{4}$ times as many.

How many cards does Dennis have?

A 75

B 60

C 50

D 45

E 30

25 Name the shape which would be formed if you connect the following co-ordinates:

(A,2) (B,4) (E,4) (F,2)

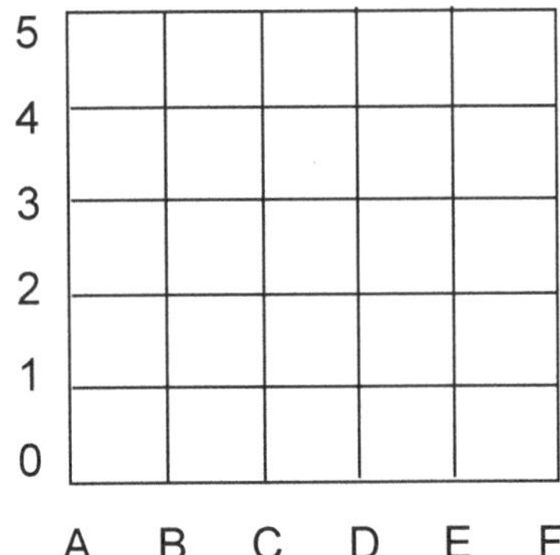

A trapezium
B rhombus
C parallelogram
D rectangle
E square

26 Portia started a quiz 12 minutes before Maria.

She had completed 5 of the 15 questions 2 minutes before Maria.

Maria finished in 1 hour.

Assuming they each worked at a consistent speed, how long did it take Portia to finish?

A 1 hour 10 minutes
B 1 hour 15 minutes
C 1 hour 20 minutes
D 1 hour 25 minutes
E 1 hour 30 minutes

Use the following graph to answer Questions **27 – 29**.

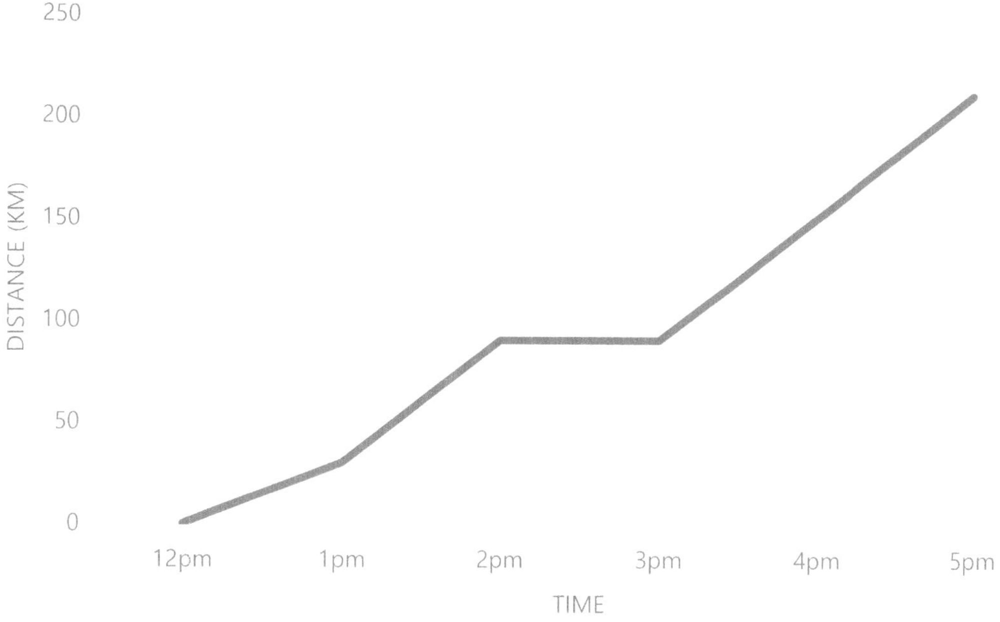

27 How long was the car **not** travelling?

A one hour
B one and a quarter hours
C one and three-quarter hours
D one and a half hours
E two hours

28 During which time was the car driving the fastest?

A 12:00 pm – 1:00 pm
B 1:00 pm – 2:00 pm
C 2:00 pm – 3:00 pm
D 12:00 pm – 4:00 pm
E 1:00 pm – 4:00 pm

29 What was the average speed for the whole trip?

A 35 km/h
B 42 km/h
C 64 km/h
D 120 km/h
E 210 km/h

30 There are 5 pink, 9 red and 6 yellow balls in a bag.

If I take one out at random, what is the probability that it is pink?

A $\frac{1}{5}$
B $\frac{3}{10}$
C $\frac{9}{20}$
D $\frac{2}{5}$
E $\frac{1}{4}$

31 In a shoe factory, it costs $10 to make the body of the shoe, $14 to make the sole, and $1 to make the shoelaces.

Each shoe is sold for 150% of its production cost, and of the profits, 80 percent goes to the owners of the company.

How much of the profit is left for the workers if 100 shoes are sold?

A $290
B $287
C $258
D $250
E $200

32 Neil has marked 24 more papers than Dennis.

If the total number of papers completed by Neil and Dennis is 84, what is the ratio of their papers, Neil to Dennis?

A 5:6

B 9:5

C 7:2

D 9:6

E 8:3

33 The total mass of 2 identical apples and 4 identical carrots is 1kg 972g.

A carrot weighs 367g.

What is the mass of one apple?

A $802\frac{1}{2}$g

B $302\frac{1}{2}$g

C 329g

D 252g

E 218g

34 Points X and Y are the centres of the two circles below.

The length of the line that runs through two centres as shown is 24 cm.

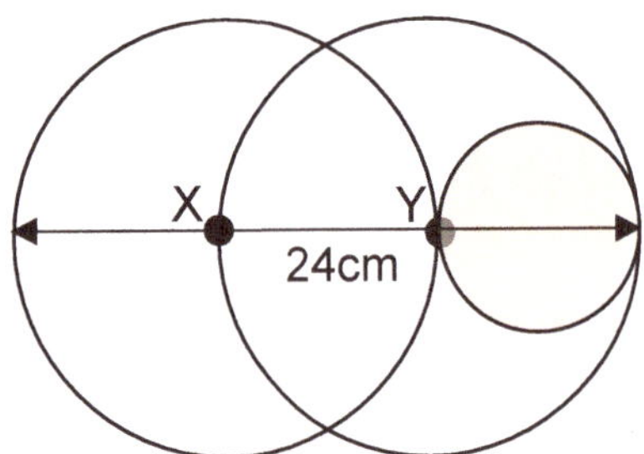

Find the area of the shaded circle. (Use π = 3.14)

A 45.76 cm squared

B 50.24 cm squared

C 62.87 cm squared

D 74.13 cm squared

E 82.14 cm squared

35 Read the information in the table below carefully.

It shows the amount of money it costs for a kilogram of rocks at different stores.

If Dennis buys 4 kilograms from each store, how much would it cost him?

Store	**Cost of Rocks ($/kilogram)**
Store A	12.20
Store B	4.10
Store C	2.00
Store D	8.35

A $75.60

B $86.60

C $92.30

D $98.70

E $106.60

Selective Practice Test

Mathematical Reasoning 7 (Time allowed: 40 min)

INSTRUCTIONS

1 Write your Name on the cover page.

2 There are 35 questions in this paper. For each question there are five possible answers, A, B, C, D and E. Choose the one correct answer and record your choice on the separate answer sheet. If you make a mistake, erase thoroughly and try again.

3 You will not lose marks for incorrect answers, so you should attempt all 35 questions

4 You must complete the answer sheet within the time limit. There will not be any extra time at the end of the exam to record your answers on the answer sheet.

5 You can use the question paper for working out, but no extra paper is allowed.

Name: ______________________________

1 The rabbit population in Sydney is given as 32 thousand rounded to the nearest thousand.

The population could be

A 31 788
B 32 722
C 33 000
D 31 499
E 320 000

2 What is the approximate size of angle *x*?

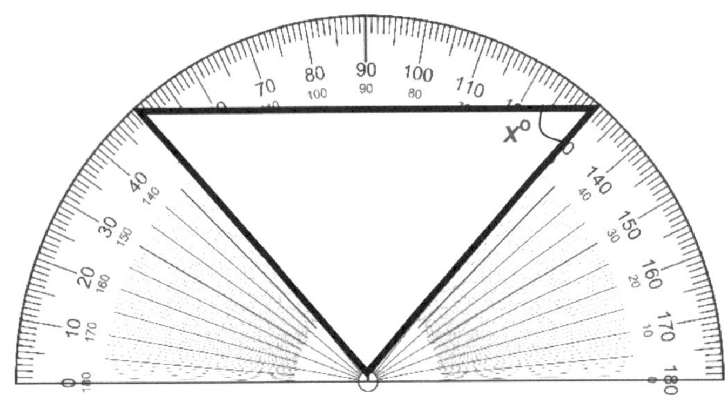

A 35°
B 40°
C 45°
D 50°
E 60°

3 A new game, Half Life 3, has just been released.

If EB Games has 33 boxes of 25 copies each, and 360 people have pre ordered copies, how many games are left to sell to customers?

A 560
B 375
C 465
D 275
E 175

4 What is the area of this floor plan?

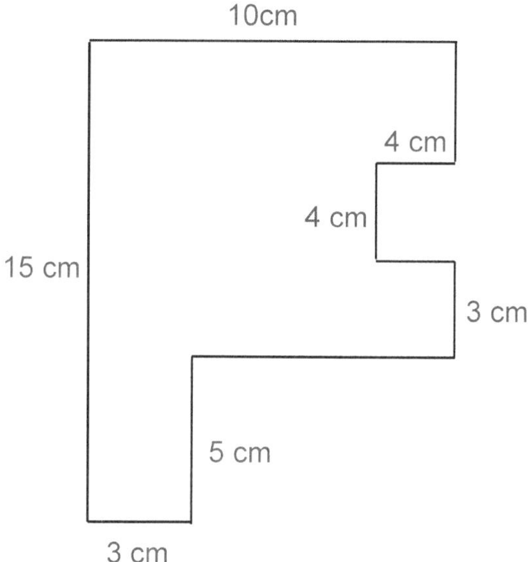

A 100 cm^2

B 99 cm^2

C 50 cm^2

D 200 cm^2

E 74 cm^2

5 Dennis has to put 5g of fertiliser on each plant for it to grow properly.

If he wants 400 plants to grow well, and each kilo of fertiliser costs 20 dollars, how much does he spend on fertiliser?

A $10

B $15

C $20

D $35

E $40

6 Out of 300 students in a school, one quarter play soccer.

Of the rest, four-fifths play T-ball.

The remaining students play tennis.

How many students play tennis?

A 225
B 180
C 100
D 75
E 45

7 Mel, Bel, Ann, Jan and Fran raced in a 400m freestyle event.

Jan finished 20 metres ahead of Bel and 25 metres ahead of Fran.

Mel finished 15 metres ahead of Ann and the distance between Ann and Jan was double the distance between Bel and Fran.

What's the difference between the first and fourth?

A 45 metres
B 50 metres
C 85 metres
D 110 metres
E 120 metres

8 Given a three-digit number (where the tens digit is not 9), the number in the tens place is increased by one.

The new number is then

A one more than the old number
B ten times the old number
C ten more than the old number
D one less than the old number
E nine more than the old number

9 Katie joined these identical pieces as shown in the diagram below.

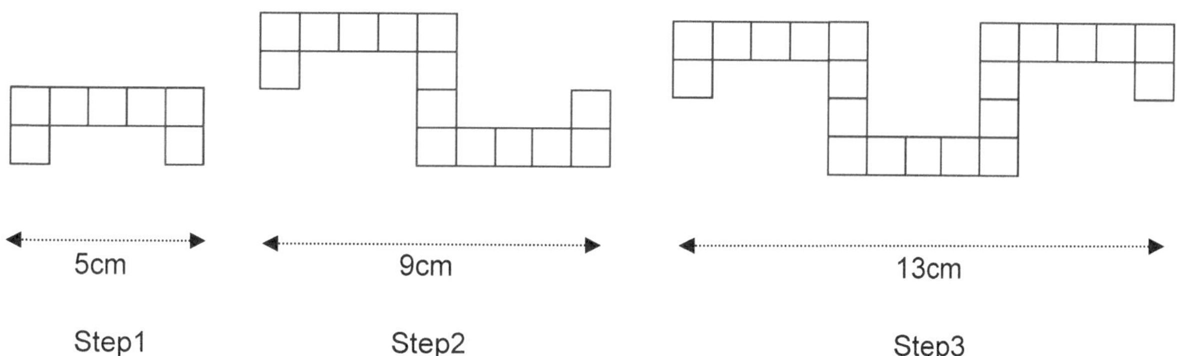

How long would Katie's shape be in Step 10?

A 41cm
B 40cm
C 38cm
D 37cm
E 21cm

10 It takes 3 sisters 3 hours and 30 minutes to sweep the monastery.

If 5 sisters were available, how long would it take to complete the task?

A 3 hours and 3 minutes
B 3 hours and 10 minutes
C 2 hours and 30 minutes
D 2 hours and 15 minutes
E 2 hours and 6 minutes

11 There is a box of 120 hair clips.

Ankita takes $\frac{1}{4}$ of the hair clips, and Jessica takes $\frac{1}{2}$ of the remainder.

If Andrew takes the rest, how many hair clips did he take?

A 15
B 30
C 45
D 60
E 90

12 Michael invested $4500 in the bank at an interest rate of 8% p.a., paid monthly.

How much money did he have in the bank after 3 months?

A $4530
B $4660
C $4550
D $4590
E $4860

13 Andrew and Neil have their whole number heights in cm with a ratio of 2:5.

Which of the following is a possible difference in their heights?

A 24 cm
B 20 cm
C 61 cm
D 26 cm
E 38 cm

Questions **14** and **15** refer to the following graph.

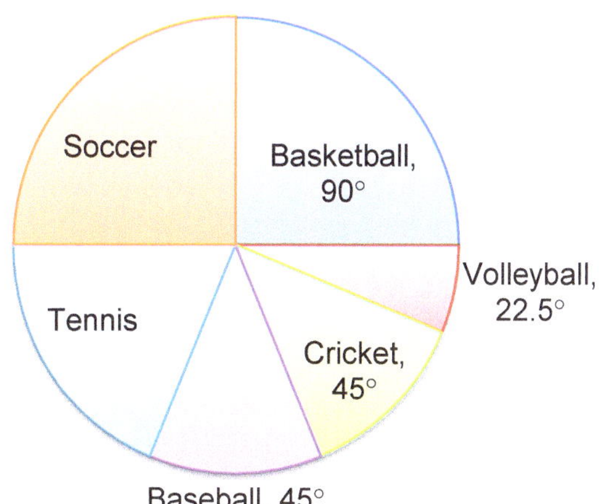

14 What percentage of students played Tennis or Volleyball?

A 12.5%
B 25%
C 37.5%
D 50%
E 90%

15 If the students that play Soccer stopped playing and half of them went to play Cricket while the other half went to play Basketball, how many students play Cricket or Basketball now?

A $\frac{3}{4}$
B $\frac{3}{5}$
C $\frac{7}{16}$
D $\frac{2}{3}$
E $\frac{5}{8}$

16 The total mass of the three boys is 156 kilograms.

Jack is 4 kilograms heavier than Sam and 8 kilograms heavier than Terry.

What is Terry's weight?

A 46 kilograms
B 48 kilograms
C 50 kilograms
D 52 kilograms
E 54 kilograms

17 For every $10 entered into a special savings account, Jessica earns 5% interest on it straight away.

How many times must Jessica deposit 10 dollars to reach $40 worth of interest?

A 100
B 90
C 80
D 70
E 60

18 What is the difference in area between a square with sides of 8 cm and a triangle with both height and base length of 12 cm?

A 8 cm^2
B 10 cm^2
C 12 cm^2
D 14 cm^2
E 16 cm^2

19 Allan took a bus to the city at a constant speed, where back and forth would take a total of 58 minutes.

If he had caught the train there and a bus back it would have taken a total of 42 minutes.

How long would it have taken to catch a train both ways?

A 26 minutes

B 35 minutes

C 36 minutes

D 45 minutes

E 75 minutes

20 What is the volume for the following shape?

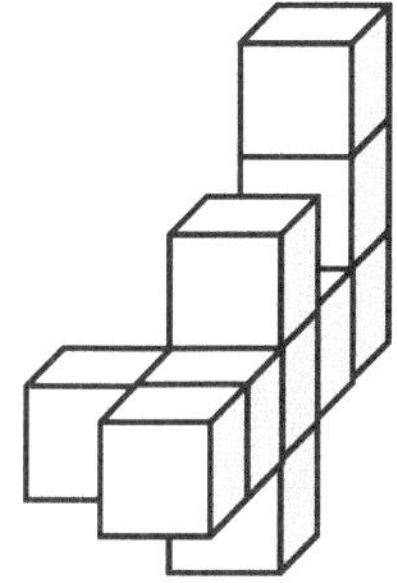

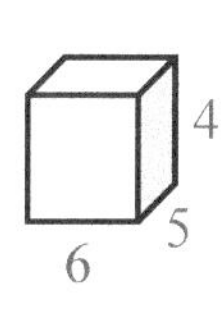

A 1400

B 1300

C 1200

D 1100

E 1000

21 Dennis and his friends were planning to start a company.

Dennis invested \$3500 in the company while Thornton invested two-fifths of that.

Neil decided to invest twice the amount Thornton invested, while Raj decided to invest five-sevenths the amount Neil invested.

If starting the company cost \$5000, how much money left over was there for other uses?

A \$4700
B \$3500
C \$9700
D \$8500
E \$6500

22 If a miner can mine 6240 kilograms of coal in a year, how many kilograms of coal does he mine each day if he works four days a week?

A 24
B 25.5
C 30
D 32.6
E 34

23 The sum of two integers (whole numbers) is taken away from their product.

The result is 41. If the numbers are consecutive, what is their sum?

A 9.
B 11.
C 15.
D 17.
E cannot be determined.

24 Harry, Hermoine and Ron all have wands.

Harry's wand has a length $\frac{6}{7}$ of Hermoine's or $\frac{6}{5}$ of Ron's length.

If Ron's wand has a length of 35cm, what is the total length of their three wands?

A 96 cm
B 106 cm
C 119 cm
D 140 cm
E 126 cm

25 All the students in Year 2 Purp are sitting in a circle.

They are all numbered sequentially.

The fifth child is seated directly opposite the twelfth child.

How many students are in Year 2 Purp?

A 12
B 14
C 16
D 18
E 20

26 Debbi is riding a bike down a road. Every time the wheels on her bike go a full rotation, she hears a loud clicking sound.

What is the full length of the ride down the road if the radius of her wheels is 28cm and she hears 20 clicks exactly? Use $\pi = \frac{22}{7}$.

A 32.8m
B 35.2m
C 44.4m
D 51.1m
E 56.0m

27 Tickets numbered 1 to 20 are mixed up and then a ticket is drawn at random.

What is the probability that the ticket drawn has a number which is a multiple of 3 or 5?

A $\frac{1}{2}$

B $\frac{2}{5}$

C $\frac{8}{15}$

D $\frac{9}{20}$

E $\frac{3}{7}$

28 Find the shape to balance the scale.

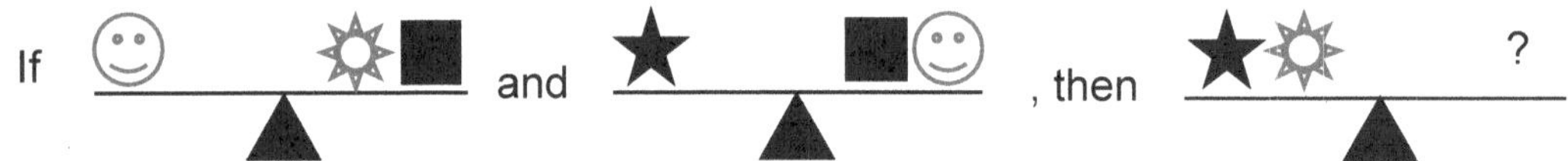

A

B

C

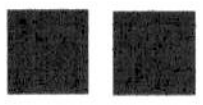

D

E

29 Lollipops cost \$0.30 each, chocolate frogs cost \$0.25 each and gummy bears cost \$0.15 each.

Lasith bought 3 lollipops, 2 chocolate frogs and a handful of gummy bears.

If he paid with two \$2 coins and received \$1.70 back in change, how many gummy bears did he buy?

A 2

B 6

C 8

D 10

E 12

30 What fraction of the rectangle below is taken up by the two triangles if their areas are separate and added?

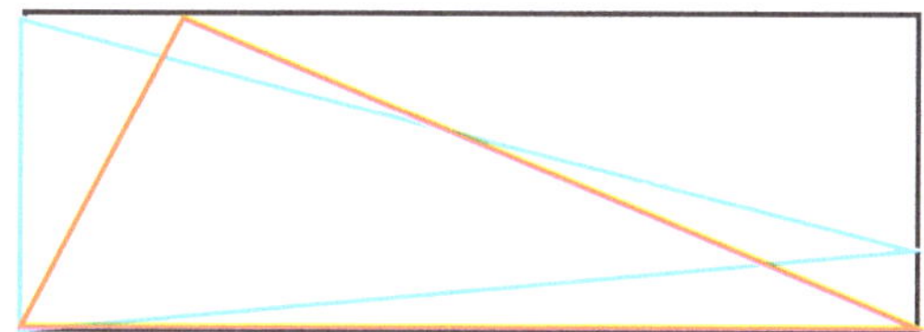

A $\frac{6}{8}$

B $\frac{7}{8}$

C $\frac{8}{8}$

D $\frac{4}{8}$

E $\frac{10}{8}$

31 Three of Julian's paces make 1.5 metres.

When he has walked 1 km how many paces has he walked?

A 1500
B 3000
C 750
D 2500
E 2000

32 A farmer wants to plant 1000 seeds on his farm land.

If each seed needs to be planted in a 40cm^2 area for it not to grow and hinder other seeds, how much farmland does the farmer need?

A 4000 m^2
B 400 m^2
C 40 m^2
D 4 m^2
E 0.4 m^2

33 The thermostat in an aquarium is broken, and the temperature initially rises by $\frac{1}{4}$ of a degree in the first hour, but the amount it rises doubles each hour.

If the temperature starts at 18 degrees and the fish will perish above 26 degrees, how many hours will it take before the fish die?

A 4 hours
B 5 hours
C 6 hours
D 7 hours
E 8 hours

34 There is a stack of one thousand pieces of cardboard, each 0.45mm thick.

What is the height of the stack in centimetres?

A 4.5
B 45
C 450
D 4500
E 45 000

35 Raymond divided his tray of brownies so that his mother got twice the amount of his sister who got two less than his dad.

Raymond got a third of the number of slices his dad got.

Which diagram shows how the brownies were divided?

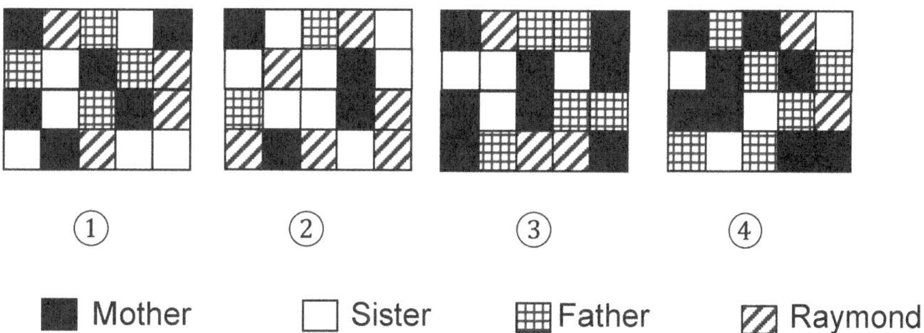

A ①
B ②
C ③
D ④
E cannot be determined.

Selective Practice Test

Mathematical Reasoning 8 (Time allowed: 40 min)

INSTRUCTIONS

1. Write your Name on the cover page.
2. There are 35 questions in this paper. For each question there are five possible answers, A, B, C, D and E. Choose the one correct answer and record your choice on the separate answer sheet. If you make a mistake, erase thoroughly and try again.
3. You will not lose marks for incorrect answers, so you should attempt all 35 questions
4. You must complete the answer sheet within the time limit. There will not be any extra time at the end of the exam to record your answers on the answer sheet.
5. You can use the question paper for working out, but no extra paper is allowed.

Name: ______________________________

1 Make the largest and the smallest possible 5 digit numbers from these digits and find the difference between them.

9, 7, 3, 8, 9

A 62874

B 62974

C 61875

D 61974

E 62074

2 Find the number of matches that are needed to build the next pattern.

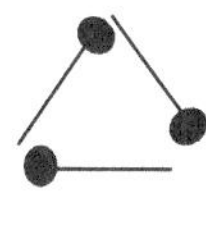
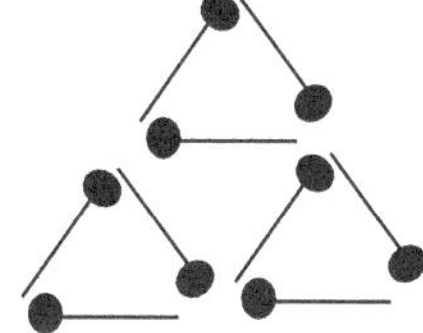
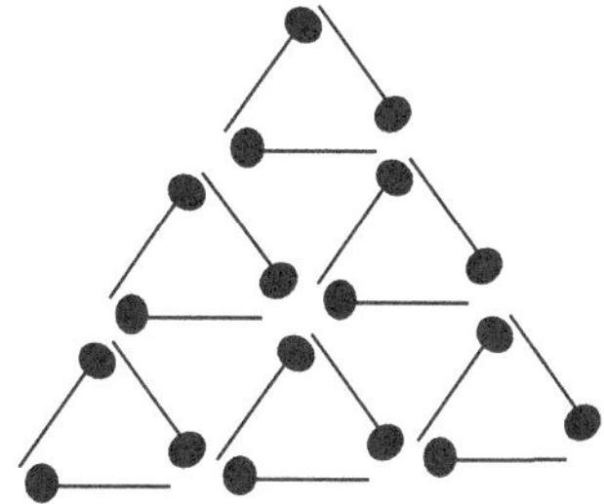

A 27

B 26

C 30

D 36

E 40

3 Mrs. Farrell was going to bake some brownies so she turned the oven control to 250°C at 11:15am.

At 11:55am the light went out, signaling that 250°C had been reached.

If the oven was initially 50°C, what was the average temperature increase per minute?

A 4.5°C

B 4.44°C

C 5.0°C

D 5.5°C

E 6.0°C

4 Twelve bottles of water were bought by Andrew, each costing $1.20 or $1.00.

If $6.40 change was received from a $20 note, how many $1.00 bottles of water were bought?

A 3
B 8
C 9
D 6
E 4

5 What is the product of $1 - \frac{3}{4}$ and $1 - \frac{1}{3}$ and $1 - \frac{2}{3}$?

A $\frac{1}{6}$
B $\frac{1}{18}$
C $\frac{1}{3}$
D $\frac{1}{4}$
E $\frac{1}{12}$

6 Kanye can say 117 words in 13 seconds. Iggy can say 164 words in 41 seconds.

If they both rap for a minute, who would have said more words, and by how much?

A Iggy, by 20 words
B Kanye, by 300 words
C Iggy, by 10 words
D Kanye, by 20 words
E Iggy, by 300 words

7 In this 10 cm by 10 cm square, A, B, C, D and E are congruent rectangles.

If the area of F is $40cm^2$, what is the area of C?

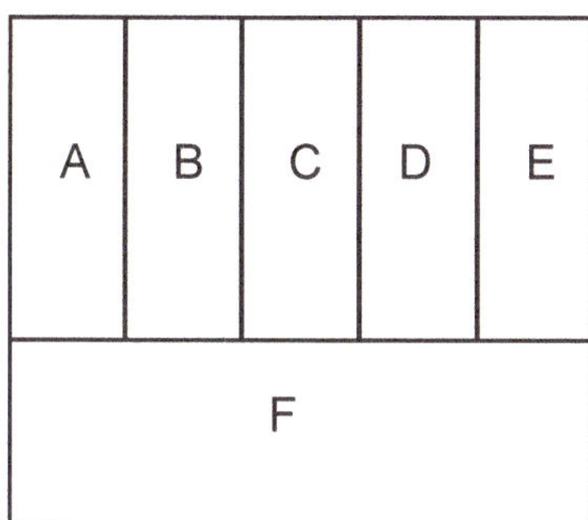

A $10\ cm^2$

B $12\ cm^2$

C $20\ cm^2$

D $24\ cm^2$

E $40\ cm^2$

8 Jonathan Fur was sleeping when he had a nightmare and suddenly woke up.

Blearily, he opened his eyes and saw this reflection of the clock in his bedside mirror.

He promptly went back to sleep.

If he woke up at 11 am, for how much longer did he sleep after waking up from his nightmare?

A 9 hours 10 minutes

B 9 hours 15 minutes

C 9 hours 20 minutes

D 9 hours 25 minutes

E 10 hours 25 minutes

9 Jeffrey purchased 5 rolls of sushi and 4 boxes of noodles.

If each box of noodles cost twice the price of a sushi roll and the total price was $32.50, how much would 2 sushi rolls and a noodle box cost?

A $5.00
B $7.50
C $8.00
D $9.00
E $10.00

10 If nine twentieths of a number is 63, then a fifth of three twenty eighths of the number is

A 4
B 16
C 15
D 3
E 9

11 This solid shape is built using small blocks. A layer of blocks is added to each face.

How many blocks are there now?

A 175
B 210
C 190
D 200
E 270

12 Dennis needs to earn 10 dollars more in his job than Andrew in order to win a bet.

If Andrew gets paid $30 an hour and works for 7 hours, which of the following will allow Dennis to win the bet most easily?

A $14 for 15 hours
B $20 for 11 hours
C $19 for 13 hours
D $20 for 10 hours
E $17 for 12 hours

13 A measuring wheel rotates 90° every 6 seconds.

How many complete revolutions would it complete in $4\frac{1}{2}$ minutes?

A 15
B 14
C 13
D 12
E 11

14

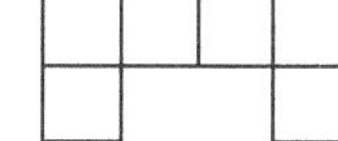

4cm long

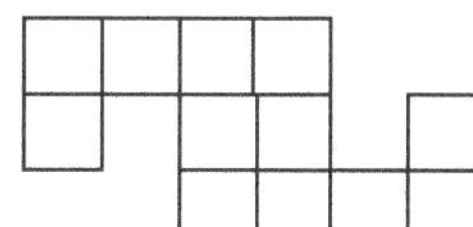

6cm long

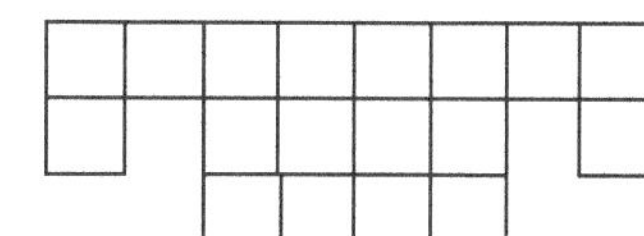

8cm long

Following the pattern above, how many of the 4cm long shapes would you need to make a shape that is 1m in length?

A 50
B 48
C 49
D 51
E 52

Questions 15 and 16 relate to the following pie graph.

15 A whole school was surveyed on their favourite movie genre.

The results are shown in the pie graph below.

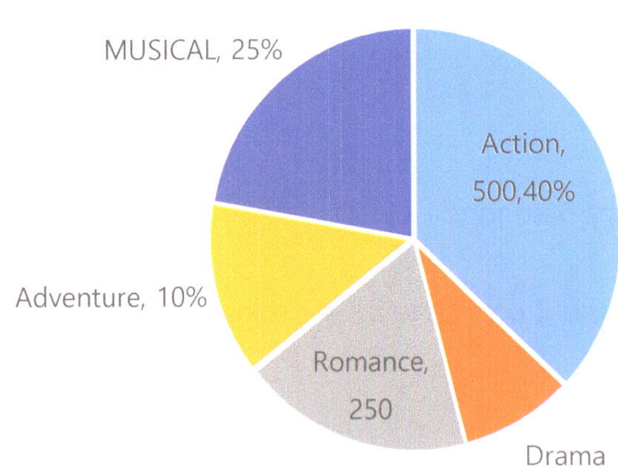

How many students picked Drama as their favourite genre?

A 5
B 13
C 42
D 62
E 82

16 A second survey was conducted; however, the genre of Action was removed.

The students that chose Action as their favourite genre in the first survey, half of them chose drama as their new favourite and half of them chose Romance.

The rest of the results remained the same between the two surveys.

How many students chose 'Drama' as their favourite genre in the second survey?

A 184
B 289
C 312
D 332
E 384

17 Peter is 18 years old, his younger brother Brian is 14 years old and their youngest brother Steven is 12.
They also have a baby sister who is one year old.
Their uncle Sean is 59 years old.

When you combine the age of all four children, how many years will their age together be over their uncle Sean's age?

A 3
B 5
C 7
D 9
E 11

18 What is the radius of the biggest circle?

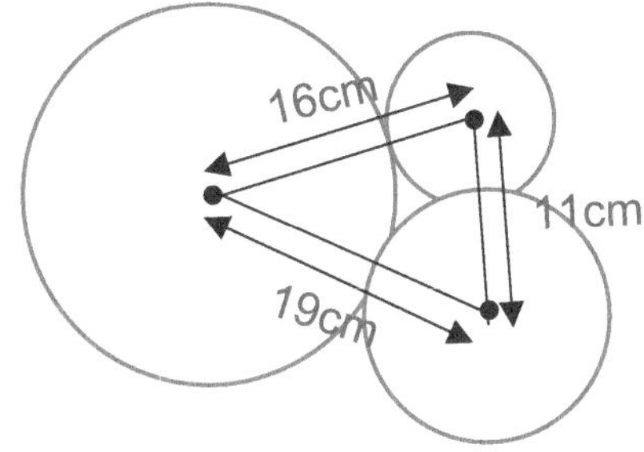

A 7cm
B 11cm
C 10cm
D 13cm
E 12cm

19 A real estate agent earns 5% commission for selling a plot of land.

If she sold a plot for $700 000, how much would the landowner receive after the agent had been paid her commission?

A $660 000
B $5 000
C $500 000
D $665 000
E $760 000

Questions **20** and **21** refer to the following graph.

This graph shows the number of apples picked by children on an excursion.

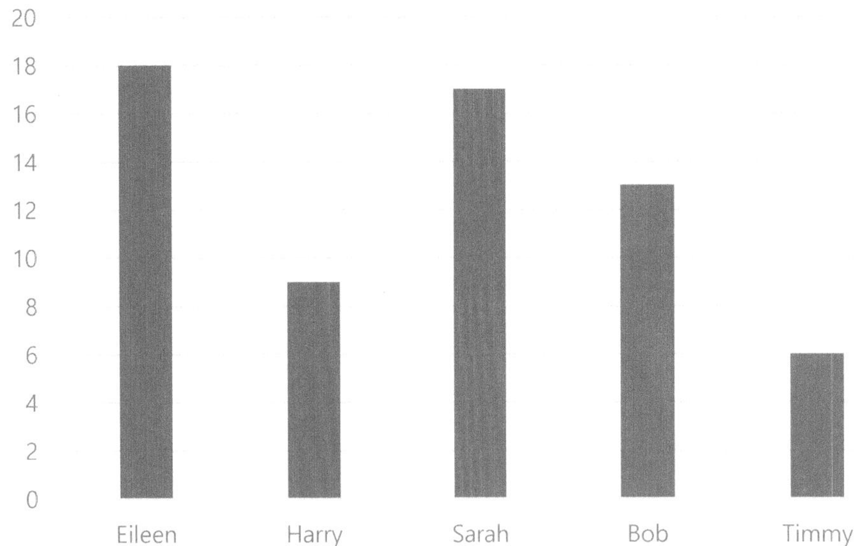

20 How many more apples did Eileen, Harry and Sarah pick than Bob and Timmy?

A 10
B 20
C 25
D 30
E 35

21 Find the average number of apples picked by each child.

Which child picked the number of apples closest to the average?

A Harry
B Sarah
C Bob
D Timmy
E Eileen

22 At a camp with 150 students, there are 7 boys to every 3 girls.

How many more boys than girls are there at camp?

A 25
B 45
C 55
D 60
E 65

23 Calculate the size of angle *x*.

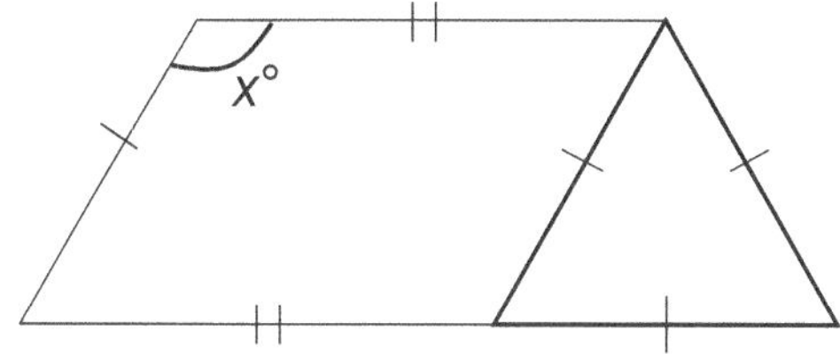

A 120°
B 115°
C 110°
D 125°
E 130°

24 A certain water through which has semicircles on each side has a radius of 10cm and length of 0.4 metres.

How much can it hold?

A 6.28L
B 628mL
C 6.82mL
D 0.682L
E 6.82L

25 Mary had 0.6 as many marbles as John, who had $\frac{5}{8}$ as many as Paul.

If Mary had 63 marbles, how many do John and Paul have combined?

A 168
B 105
C 126
D 186
E 273

26 Alan bought 1 pack of chips and 2 chocolate bars for $5.80

Andrew bought 3 packs of chips and 2 chocolate bars for $10.20

If both of them bought the chips and chocolate bars from the same store, what is the price of 1 pack of chips and 1 chocolate bar?

A $1.80
B $2.20
C $3.80
D $4.00
E $4.20

27 Sara wants to make a box without a lid. For the box, she starts with a piece of cardboard with a length of 10 centimetres and a width is 8 centimetres.

Then she cuts congruent squares with a side of 2 centimetres at the four corners.

What is the area of paper needed for the box without a lid?

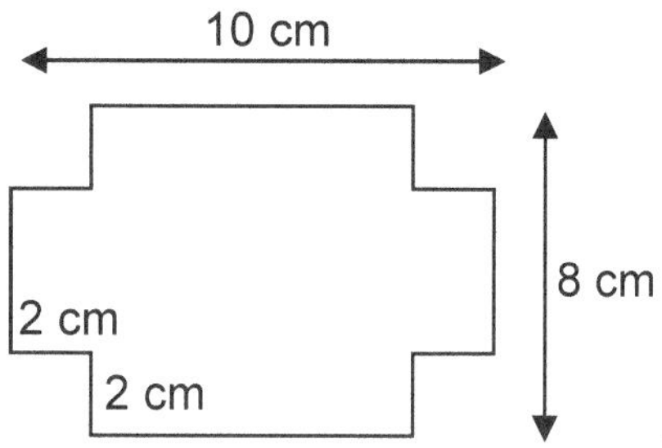

A 62 cm²

B 64 cm²

C 68 cm²

D 78 cm²

E 82 cm²

28 A certain fraction is greater than $1\frac{1}{8}$ and less than $1\frac{2}{5}$.

If the denominator of this fraction is 40, how many possible values are there for the numerator?

A 1

B 3

C 10

D 11

E 20

29 A group of children are sharing toys.

If each child receives 10 toys they are short 5 toys, but if each child gets 8 toys there are 15 left over. How many children are sharing the toys?

A 9
B 10
C 11
D 12
E 13

30 Find the value of ★ + ☆ + ○ + ♣

If ★ + ○ = 14,
★ − ○ = 12,
♣ = ☆ + ☆ + ☆+ ☆
and ★ + ★ + ○ + ♣ + ♣ = 43

A 24
B 36
C 18
D 30
E 20

Questions **31** and **32** use the following information.

This is a 6 × 6 centimetre squre.

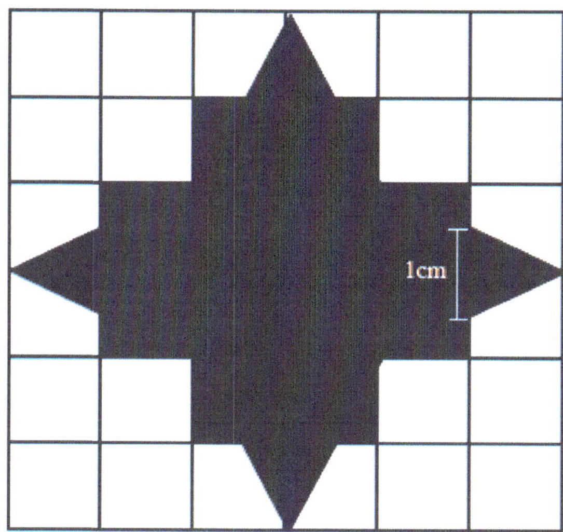

31 Calculate the area of $\frac{1}{2}$ the shaded star.

A 6 cm^2

B 7 cm^2

C 14 cm^2

D 12 cm^2

E 9 cm^2

32 What fraction of the 6 × 6 centimetre square is covered by the star?

A $\frac{1}{2}$

B $\frac{2}{5}$

C $\frac{7}{18}$

D $\frac{4}{17}$

E $\frac{4}{7}$

33 At a school of 800 people, 50% have black eyes and 10% have green eyes.

Of the remainder, 25% have blue eyes and the rest have brown eyes.

How many have brown eyes?

A 400
B 240
C 160
D 80
E 40

34 James started running laps from Monday to Sunday.

The number of metres he runs increases 50m every day.

If by Sunday he runs 400m, how far has he run in total at the end of Friday?

A 790m
B 800m
C 850m
D 900m
E 1000m

35 Roger has four different shirts, six different pairs of pants, and three different pairs of shoes.

How many distinct outfits can he make?

A 36
B 48
C 56
D 63
E 72

Selective Practice Test

Mathematical Reasoning 9 (Time allowed: 40 min)

INSTRUCTIONS

1. Write your Name on the cover page.
2. There are 35 questions in this paper. For each question there are five possible answers, A, B, C, D and E. Choose the one correct answer and record your choice on the separate answer sheet. If you make a mistake, erase thoroughly and try again.
3. You will not lose marks for incorrect answers, so you should attempt all 35 questions
4. You must complete the answer sheet within the time limit. There will not be any extra time at the end of the exam to record your answers on the answer sheet.
5. You can use the question paper for working out, but no extra paper is allowed.

Name: ______________________________

1 Add three quarters of a hundred thousand to six hundred and sixty-nine thousand seven hundred and eight. The result is

A 744208.
B 744302.
C 744708.
D 744710.
E 744808.

2 Clive stands facing East, then he makes a 45°-turn anti-clockwise, then another turn 180° anticlockwise.

What direction is Clive facing now?

A North-East
B North-West
C West
D South-West
E East

3 A jar of milk has a mass of 2000 grams.

A third of the milk and the jar weigh 1000 grams.

Calculate the mass of the jar.

A 420 grams
B 495 grams
C 500 grams
D 505 grams
E 510 grams

4 Which of the following will give the largest number?

A $3 \times 10^3 + 5 \times 10^3$

B $5 \times 10^5 + 8 \times 10^6$

C $6 \times 10^5 + 2 \times 10^5$

D $20 \times 10^4 + 2 \times 10^3$

E $4 \times 10^6 + 5 \times 10^6$

5 Daniel, Tom and Hodie share $270 in this way.

Hodie gets $40 more than Tom and Hodie receives $20 more than Daniel.

How much did Hodie get?

A $70.00

B $90.00

C $100.00

D $110.00

E $120.00

6 What is the area of the following shape?

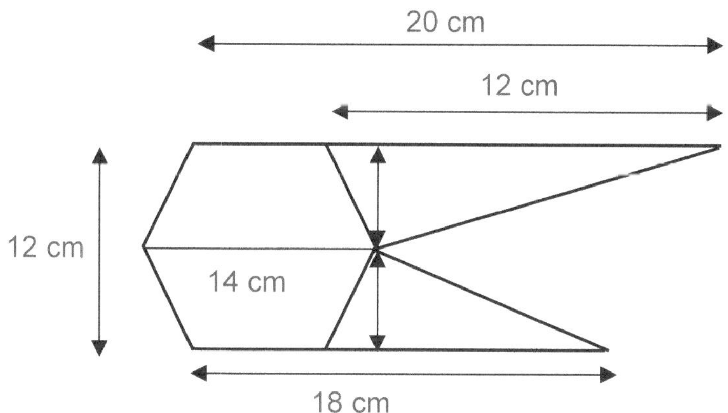

A 197 cm^2

B 198 cm^2

C 199 cm^2

D 200 cm^2

E 210 cm^2

7 Dennis bought some chocolates at the confectionary for $9.00, some at 60 cents each and some at 30 cents each.

He bought 6 less of the cheaper chocolates.

How many 30 cents of chocolates did Dennis buy?

A 3
B 4
C 6
D 8
E 9

8 At the bus stop Sam counted the colours of trucks that passed him.

A quarter were silver, $\frac{1}{3}$ were white, $\frac{1}{6}$ were yellow, $\frac{1}{9}$ were red and there were 5 black trucks.

How many trucks did Sam count?

A 32
B 36
C 48
D 56
E 64

9 A + B + C = 15 and B + C + D = 18

If A, B, C and D are all consecutive numbers, what is the value of C?

A 5
B 6
C 7
D 8
E 9

Questions 10 and 11 use the following information.

Turf can be bought in rolls 50 centimetres by two metres.

10 How many rolls would be needed to cover an area 24 metres square?

A 12
B 24
C 36
D 40
E 62

11 A roll costs $1.25. How much to turf the 24-metre square area?

A $22
B $25
C $28
D $30
E $32

12 Simon bought a new computer set costing $3220.

He paid $1000 as a down payment and will pay off the remainder in 12 months.

How much will Simon have to pay per month?

A $165
B $170
C $175
D $181
E $185

Questions 13, 14, 15 and 16 use the following information.

The graph shows two cars travelling to the same destination along the same route.

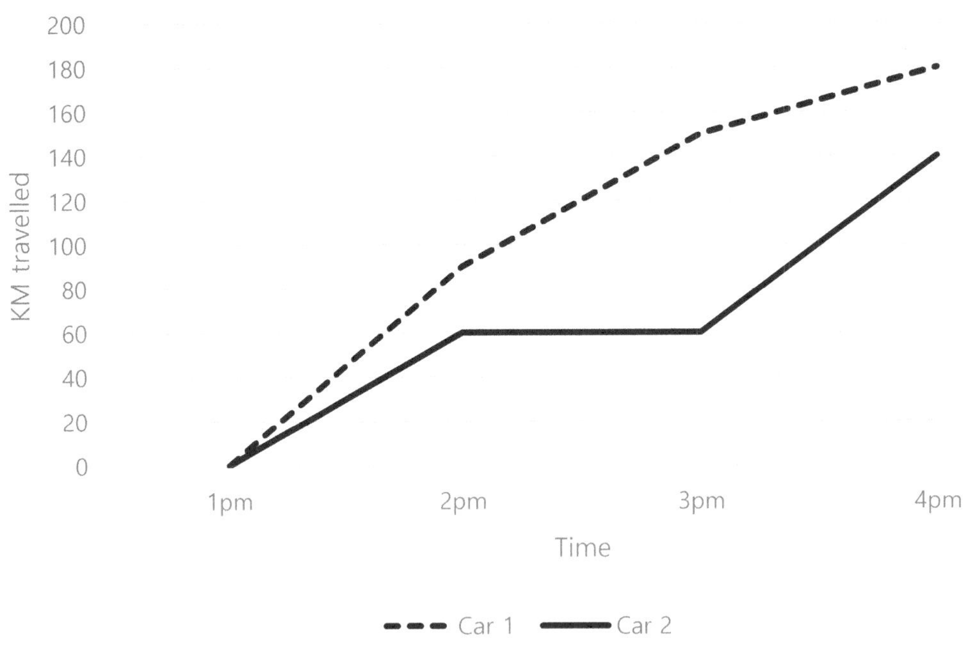

13 When Car 2 stopped at 2 pm how far had Car 1 travelled?

A 80 kilometres

B 90 kilometres

C 100 kilometres

D 110 kilometres

E 120 kilometres

14 For how much more time during the trip did Car 2 stop than Car 1?

A 30 minutes

B 45 minutes

C one hour

D $1\frac{1}{2}$ hours

E two hours

15 Between one o'clock and three o'clock what was Car 1's average speed?

A 60 kilometres per hour
B 65 kilometres per hour
C 70 kilometres per hour
D 75 kilometres per hour
E 80 kilometres per hour

16 During which times did Car 2 travel at an average speed of 40 kilometres per hour?

A 1pm $\rightarrow$ 2pm
B 1pm $\rightarrow$ 3pm
C 1pm $\rightarrow$ 4pm
D 3pm $\rightarrow$ 4pm
E 2pm $\rightarrow$ 4pm

17 A container that is $\frac{2}{5}$ full holds 150ml of water.

How much more water is needed for the container to be two thirds full?

A 75 mL
B 100 mL
C 125 mL
D 175 mL
E 250 mL

18 If 

Then what is the weight of ★?

A 5 grams
B 10 grams
C 15 grams
D 20 grams
E 25 grams

19 If the ages of Dave and Dale are multiplied together, the answer is 121.

What is the total of their ages?

A 18
B 22
C 24
D 26
E 28

20 A soccer team won 16 out of their 24 matches. Three-quarters of the wins were won by more than two goals.

What percentage of all the matches were won by more than two goals?

A 40%
B 42%
C 45%
D 50%
E 60%

21 An insurance company paid Hannah $3 150 for her stolen laptop.

If the payment was only 70% of its value, what was the original value of the laptop?

A $3 500
B $4 000
C $4 500
D $5 000
E $6 500

22 Dylan has been doing well in his tests out of 100. He has scored 52, 66, 70 and 75.

Dylan wants his average after the next test to be 70.

What will he have to score on that test to reach his goal?

A 72
B 76
C 80
D 82
E 87

Questions 23 and 24 use the following information.

Jonathan is making a path 0.5 metres wide by 3.5 metres long using black and white tiles.

This is the pattern being used to make the path. Each pattern is 7 cm x 25 cm in size.

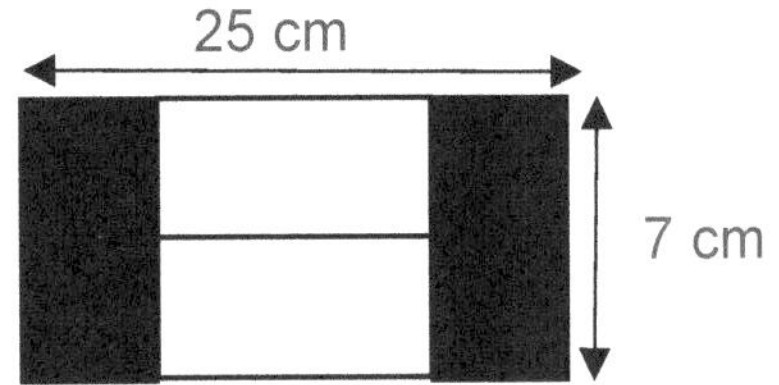

23 How many black tiles are needed?

A 100
B 200
C 300
D 400
E 500

24 The tiles are the same price, costing $9.50 for a box of 10 tiles.

How much will it cost Jonathan to lay his path?

A $380.00
B $395.00
C $400.00
D $450.00
E $520.00

25 Seven consecutive numbers have a total of 210.

When one of the numbers is removed, the average stays the same as the average of the original numbers.

Which is the number?

A 28
B 30
C 32
D 35
E 38

26 The shape below contains 4 regular hexagons.

What is the perimeter of the shape if each side is 4.5cm?

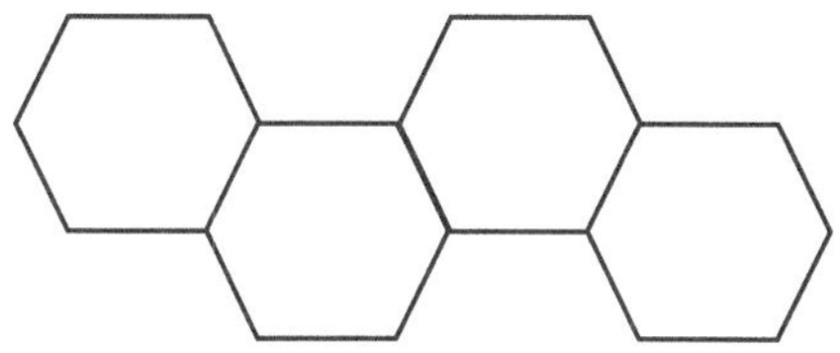

A 81 cm
B 90 cm
C 93 cm
D 99 cm
E 108 cm

27 If the shaded shape is equal to 3 units, find the area of the following shape.

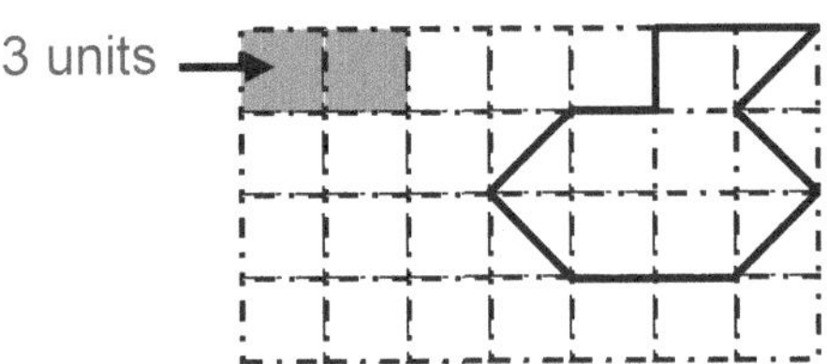

A 11.25 units squared
B 12.25 units squared
C 13.25 units squared
D 14.25 units squared
E 15.25 units squared

28 In Benji's classroom there are 4 desks behind him and 3 in front of him.

There are 4 desks to Benji's left and 5 to his right.

If all rows and columns are full, how many desks are in the room?

A 64
B 72
C 80
D 90
E 96

29 A concrete mixture is made up of metal:sand:cement in the ratio 1:2:7 respectively.

How much cement is needed for 450 kg of concrete?

A 450 kg
B 315 kg
C 285 kg
D 275 kg
E 250 kg

30 Dan and Dom take 5 hours to both pump water into a pool.

If Dom gets another friend to help them and they all pump at the same rate, how much time will they save?

A 2 hours
B 1 hour 10 minutes
C 1 hour 20 minutes
D 1 hour 30 minutes
E 1 hour 40 minutes

31 If ♠ + ♠ + ♠ + ♣ = 26.5
and ♠ + ♠ + ♣ = 19.1
then ♣ = ?

A 4.3
B 5.0
C 6.4
D 7.4
E 8.1

32 There were 30 students in the library.

Three boys left and 9 more girls came in.

There are now three times as many girls in the library as boys.

How many of the original 30 students were boys?

A 10
B 12
C 14
D 16
E 18

33 Find the volume of a cylinder that has a height of 10cm, and a circular base radius of 5cm. (π= 3.14)

A 314 cm^3
B 157 cm^3
C 550 cm^3
D 785 cm^3
E 895 cm^3

34 At MYER, there was a 30% discount on all items except for those with existing discounts.

If Neil bought a sweater that cost $110 with a 20% discount, a wallet that cost $80 with a 40% discount, and a pair of jeans at $50, how much did he pay in total?

A $435
B $455
C $255
D $171
E $150

35 A certain virus doubles itself everyday.

When one of these bacteria is placed in a petri dish, in 10 days the petri dish becomes exactly full.

If 16 of these viruses were placed in the petri dish, how many days will the petri dish be full?

A 2 days
B 3 days
C 4 days
D 5 days
E 6 days

Selective Practice Test

Mathematical Reasoning 10 (Time allowed: 40 min)

INSTRUCTIONS

1. Write your Name on the cover page.
2. There are 35 questions in this paper. For each question there are five possible answers, A, B, C, D and E. Choose the one correct answer and record your choice on the separate answer sheet. If you make a mistake, erase thoroughly and try again.
3. You will not lose marks for incorrect answers, so you should attempt all 35 questions
4. You must complete the answer sheet within the time limit. There will not be any extra time at the end of the exam to record your answers on the answer sheet.
5. You can use the question paper for working out, but no extra paper is allowed.

Name: ______________________________

1 A score was added to the set of scores below.

5 5 7 8 8

The new average is 6.

What score was added?

A 1
B 2
C 3
D 4
E 5

2 An even number squared added to an even number squared will always equal

A a prime number.
B a square number.
C a cube number.
D an odd number.
E an even number.

3 A countdown sign in the shopping centre reminds me there are still 92 days until Christmas, 2020.

If today is Monday, what day will Christmas in 2020 fall on?

A Sunday
B Monday
C Tuesday
D Wednesday
E Friday

4 A fraction is less than eight-elevenths but greater than thirty-one-forty-fourths.

The fraction's denominator is 88.

What is its numerator?

A 61
B 63
C 65
D 78
E 80

5 Jessica has the same number of ten-cent coins as she has fifty-cent coins.

If their total value is $15, how many coins does Jessica have altogether?

A 50 coins
B 55 coins
C 60 coins
D 65 coins
E 70 coins

6 In five years' time, Zara will be half the age of her mother Indira.

Indira gave birth to Zara when she was 24 years old.

How old is Indira now?

A 39
B 24
C 41
D 43
E 45

7 Luna had $\frac{2}{5}$, and Celeste had $\frac{1}{9}$ of a pizza.

Then 2 of their friends shared the leftovers.

How much did each of the friends get?

A $\frac{5}{48}$

B $\frac{7}{12}$

C $\frac{11}{45}$

D $\frac{12}{43}$

E $\frac{1}{4}$

8 What is the reflex angle between the hands of a clock at 8?

A 300°
B 120°
C 315°
D 240°
E 270°

9 To encourage themselves to lose weight, Alan, Ian, Patricia, Silvia and Nicolas each put $50 into a pot.

They weighed themselves when they began and again at the end of each week.

The one who had lost the most weight after 4 weeks won $250.

The following chart shows their progress:

	Alan	Ian	Patricia	Silvia	Nicolas
Starting weight	80 kg	91 kg	64.5 kg	60.5 kg	110 kg
Weight after week 1	78 kg	90 kg	62 kg	59 kg	107 kg
Weight after week 2	77 kg	85 kg	59 kg	56.5 kg	104 kg
Weight after week 3	73 kg	82 kg	57.5 kg	54 kg	100 kg
Weight after week 4	72 kg	79 kg	56.5 kg	55 kg	97 kg

Who won the $250?

A Alan
B Ian
C Patricia
D Silvia
E Nicolas

10 What amount cannot be made with five 10-cent coins, three 20-cent coins, and one 50-cent coin?

A $1.20
B $0.50
C $0.95
D $1.00
E $1.60

11 The ratio of green to red jellybeans in a packet is 6:15.

If there are 54 green jellybeans in the packet, how many red jellybeans are there?

A 125

B 135

C 118

D 108

E 96

12 What fraction of the following shape is shaded?

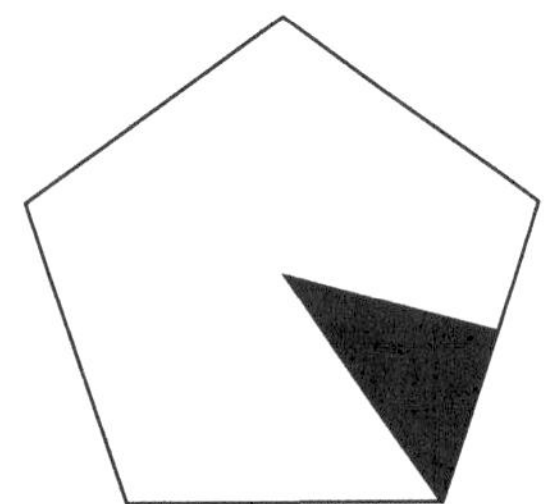

A $\frac{1}{10}$

B $\frac{1}{8}$

C $\frac{1}{12}$

D $\frac{1}{9}$

E $\frac{1}{6}$

13 Four-fifths of a pole is below the ground and 17 metres is above the ground.

How many metres short of 110 metres is the pole?

A 37.5 metres

B 40 metres

C 25 metres

D $65\frac{1}{2}$ metres

E 45 metres

14 Alice was told to think of a number, add 6, then divide by 12, and finally subtract the result from 290.

Unfortunately, instead of adding 6, she mistakenly subtracted 6, with her resulting number being 271.

If she had followed the instructions carefully, what would have been her result?

A 270

B 273

C 276

D 279

E 280

15 Small cubes have been assembled to build this 3D shape.

It has then been completely painted on all sides.

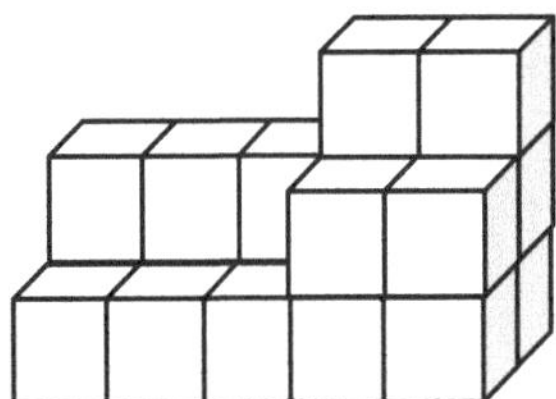

How many cubes have only three of their faces painted?

A 13

B 11

C 4

D 7

E 9

16 If the 4th number in a pattern is 4 and the ninth number is 1, what is the 6th number?

A 3.0

B 2.6

C 3.2

D 3.4

E 2.8

17 If all the corners were cut off a hexagonal pyramid, the number of faces would now be the same as

A an octagonal prism.

B a dodecagonal prism.

C a heptagonal pyramid.

D a cube.

E a pentagonal pyramid.

18 3 builders can build half a wall in 2 days.

How long will it take 6 builders to build a whole wall?

A 1 day
B 2 days
C 4 days
D 6 days
E 8 days

19 Rice can be bought in different quantities.

What would be the best buy?

A 500 g for $2.10
B 1.5 kg for $4.85
C 750 g for $2.55
D 1.0 kg for $3.29
E 2.0 kg for $5.00

20 When all the students doing Lucy's course are put into groups of 7, there are 6 students left over.

When put into groups of 8, there is one student left over.

If there are less than 160 students in Lucy's course, how many students will be left over if the class is put into groups of 3?

A 7
B 3
C 4
D 2
E None

21 A certain parallelogram-shaped pool has a width of 10 metres and a length of 14 metres.

Surrounding it is a garden spanning 3 metres away from each side of the pool.

What is the total area of the pool and garden combined?

A 220 m^2

B 320 m^2

C 240 m^2

D 250 m^2

E 300 m^2

22 What is the volume of the figure below if each side of the small cube is 2cm?

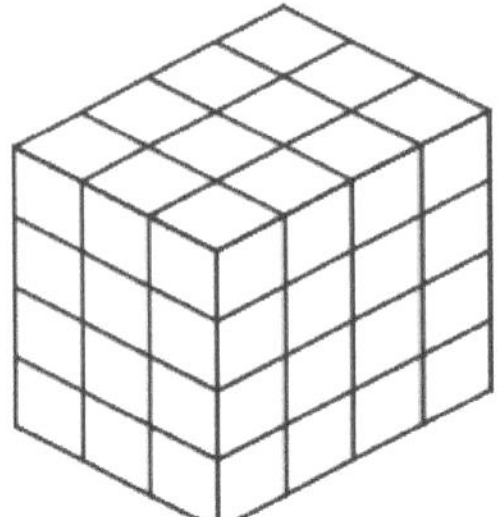

A 48 cm^3

B 96 cm^3

C 192 cm^3

D 384 cm^3

E 432 cm^3

23 Andrew borrowed $10000 from his rich friend Dennis.

If he pays off 10% of the original borrowed amount every year, how much would he still owe after 4 years?

A $1000

B $4000

C $6000

D $8000

E $9960

24 Krishni is on a diet. On Sunday, she eats 10kg of food, and every following day she eats 10% less food than the amount she ate the previous day.

What percentage of the original amount of food does Krishni eat on Wednesday?

A 73%

B 70%

C 67%

D 63%

E 60%

Questions 25 and 26 use the following information.

The pie graph shows the proportion of goals scored during the soccer season by five children.

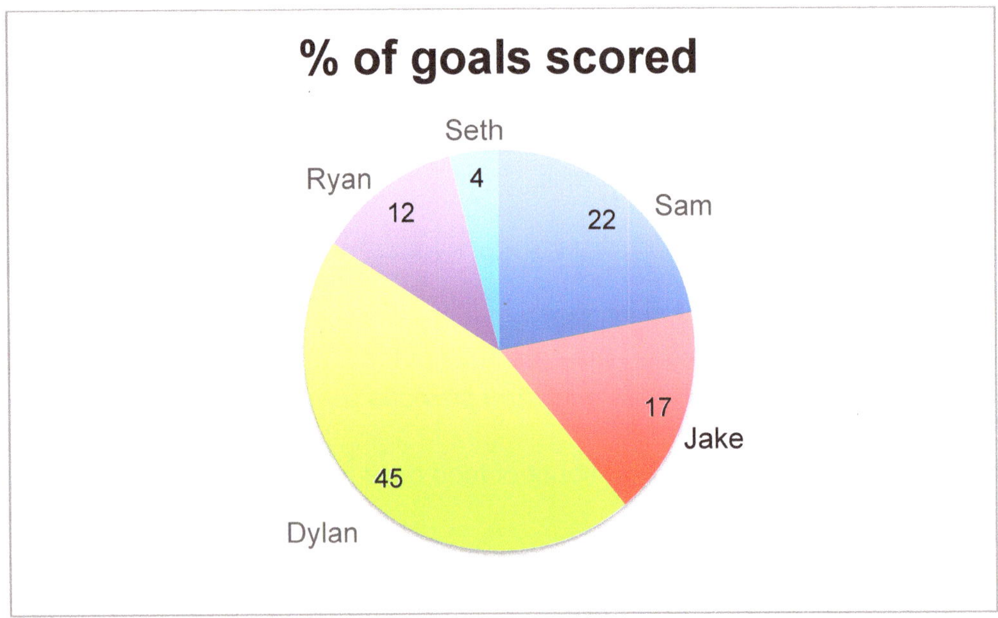

25 Ryan scored 3 times as many goals as Seth.

If Seth scored 16 goals, how many did Dylan score?

A 180
B 48
C 56
D 62
E 120

26 If Jake scored 51 goals, how many goals did Sam score?

A 45
B 66
C 96
D 78
E 58

27 What is the interest earned on $20000 at $4\frac{2}{5}$% p.a. for 24 months?

A $176
B $8800
C $880
D $1760
E $1880

28 The diameter of the circle below is 6 cm.

What is the area of the shaded part? (Use π = 3.14)

A 3.14 cm^2
B 7.74 cm^2
C 28.26 cm^2
D 56.24 cm^2
E 113.04 cm^2

29 Eric has a spinner that is split into five equal sections.

He spins the spinner and it lands on 4.

Now Ian is going to spin the spinner once. Which of these statements is/are correct?

X The probability of Ian getting a 4 is 20%
Y The probability that Ian's number is more than Eric's is 40%
Z The probability that Ian and Eric's scores add up to make more than 6 is $\frac{1}{2}$

A none of them
B statements X and Y only
C statements X and Z only
D statements Y and Z only
E statements X, Y and Z

30 Two taps are filling up a 3.6 kilolitre capacity tank.

One of the taps is filling the tank at a rate of 5 L every 5 seconds, while the second tap allows 4 L of water into the tank every 4 seconds.

How long will it take to fill the tank?

A 18 minutes
B 25 minutes
C 30 minutes
D 45 minutes
E 60 minutes

31 What shape do you form when you join the coordinates (-3,0), (0,3), (4,0) and (0,-4)?

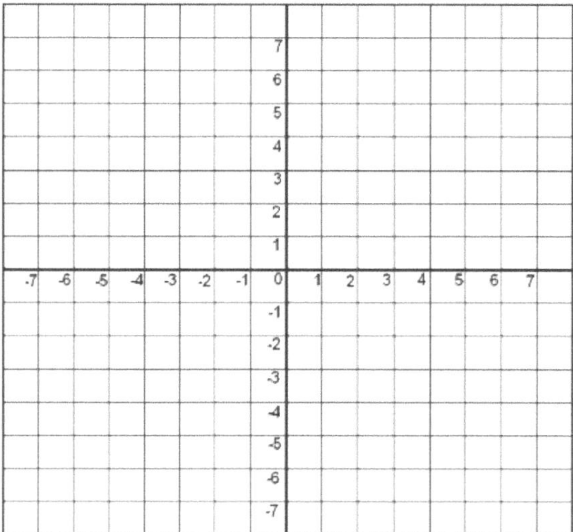

A square

B parallelogram

C rectangle

D rhombus

E trapezium

32 A ball was dropped from 6 metres high. Bounces come up to a third of the height it fell from.

By how much did the height of the ball decrease after the third bounce, in terms of metres?

A $\frac{2}{3}$m

B $\frac{2}{9}$m

C 2m

D $5\frac{7}{9}$m

E 4m

33 If you add 50 to 10^4 and add the digits in the answer, the sum of those digits is

A 6

B 9

C 16

D 5

E 11

Questions 34 and 35 use the following information.

Wallace lives in the town of Baulkham Hills, while his son Grommit resides 35 km due west in St Mary's.

34 Wallace is facing south. He turns 135° anticlockwise.

How much and in which direction must he turn so he is facing St Mary's?

A 45° anti-clockwise

B 90° clockwise

C 135° clockwise

D 135° anti-clockwise

E 270° clockwise

35 Wallace and Grommit decide to meet each other between Baulkham Hills and St Mary's.

They set off from their respective hometowns towards each other at the same time.

If Wallace walks at the speed of 4 km/h and Walter 3 km/h, after how many hours will they meet?

A 2 hours

B 3 hours

C 4 hours

D 5 hours

E 6 hours

Selective High School Practice Test
Mathematical Reasoning 6 – Answer Sheet

Fill in the appropriate circle for your chosen answer

Eg.. A B C D E
○ ● ○ ○ ○

Use a pencil. If you make a mistake, erase thoroughly and try again.

NAME : **SCORE:**

1	A B C D E ○○○○○	8	A B C D E ○○○○○	15	A B C D E ○○○○○	22	A B C D E ○○○○○	29	A B C D E ○○○○○
2	A B C D E ○○○○○	9	A B C D E ○○○○○	16	A B C D E ○○○○○	23	A B C D E ○○○○○	30	A B C D E ○○○○○
3	A B C D E ○○○○○	10	A B C D E ○○○○○	17	A B C D E ○○○○○	24	A B C D E ○○○○○	31	A B C D E ○○○○○
4	A B C D E ○○○○○	11	A B C D E ○○○○○	18	A B C D E ○○○○○	25	A B C D E ○○○○○	32	A B C D E ○○○○○
5	A B C D E ○○○○○	12	A B C D E ○○○○○	19	A B C D E ○○○○○	26	A B C D E ○○○○○	33	A B C D E ○○○○○
6	A B C D E ○○○○○	13	A B C D E ○○○○○	20	A B C D E ○○○○○	27	A B C D E ○○○○○	34	A B C D E ○○○○○
7	A B C D E ○○○○○	14	A B C D E ○○○○○	21	A B C D E ○○○○○	28	A B C D E ○○○○○	35	A B C D E ○○○○○

BLANK PAGE

Selective High School Practice Test
Mathematical Reasoning 7 – Answer Sheet

Fill in the appropriate circle for your chosen answer

Eg.. A B C D E
○ ● ○ ○ ○

Use a pencil. If you make a mistake, erase thoroughly and try again.

NAME : **SCORE:**

1 A B C D E ○○○○○	8 A B C D E ○○○○○	15 A B C D E ○○○○○	22 A B C D E ○○○○○	29 A B C D E ○○○○○
2 A B C D E ○○○○○	9 A B C D E ○○○○○	16 A B C D E ○○○○○	23 A B C D E ○○○○○	30 A B C D E ○○○○○
3 A B C D E ○○○○○	10 A B C D E ○○○○○	17 A B C D E ○○○○○	24 A B C D E ○○○○○	31 A B C D E ○○○○○
4 A B C D E ○○○○○	11 A B C D E ○○○○○	18 A B C D E ○○○○○	25 A B C D E ○○○○○	32 A B C D E ○○○○○
5 A B C D E ○○○○○	12 A B C D E ○○○○○	19 A B C D E ○○○○○	26 A B C D E ○○○○○	33 A B C D E ○○○○○
6 A B C D E ○○○○○	13 A B C D E ○○○○○	20 A B C D E ○○○○○	27 A B C D E ○○○○○	34 A B C D E ○○○○○
7 A B C D E ○○○○○	14 A B C D E ○○○○○	21 A B C D E ○○○○○	28 A B C D E ○○○○○	35 A B C D E ○○○○○

BLANK PAGE

Selective High School Practice Test
Mathematical Reasoning 8 – Answer Sheet

Fill in the appropriate circle for your chosen answer

Eg.. A B C D E
○ ● ○ ○ ○

Use a pencil. If you make a mistake, erase thoroughly and try again.

NAME : **SCORE:**

1	A B C D E ○○○○○	8	A B C D E ○○○○○	15	A B C D E ○○○○○	22	A B C D E ○○○○○	29	A B C D E ○○○○○
2	A B C D E ○○○○○	9	A B C D E ○○○○○	16	A B C D E ○○○○○	23	A B C D E ○○○○○	30	A B C D E ○○○○○
3	A B C D E ○○○○○	10	A B C D E ○○○○○	17	A B C D E ○○○○○	24	A B C D E ○○○○○	31	A B C D E ○○○○○
4	A B C D E ○○○○○	11	A B C D E ○○○○○	18	A B C D E ○○○○○	25	A B C D E ○○○○○	32	A B C D E ○○○○○
5	A B C D E ○○○○○	12	A B C D E ○○○○○	19	A B C D E ○○○○○	26	A B C D E ○○○○○	33	A B C D E ○○○○○
6	A B C D E ○○○○○	13	A B C D E ○○○○○	20	A B C D E ○○○○○	27	A B C D E ○○○○○	34	A B C D E ○○○○○
7	A B C D E ○○○○○	14	A B C D E ○○○○○	21	A B C D E ○○○○○	28	A B C D E ○○○○○	35	A B C D E ○○○○○

BLANK PAGE

Selective High School Practice Test Mathematical Reasoning 9 – Answer Sheet

Fill in the appropriate circle for your chosen answer

Eg.. A B C D E
○ ● ○ ○ ○

Use a pencil. If you make a mistake, erase thoroughly and try again.

NAME : **SCORE:**

1 A B C D E ○○○○○	8 A B C D E ○○○○○	15 A B C D E ○○○○○	22 A B C D E ○○○○○	29 A B C D E ○○○○○
2 A B C D E ○○○○○	9 A B C D E ○○○○○	16 A B C D E ○○○○○	23 A B C D E ○○○○○	30 A B C D E ○○○○○
3 A B C D E ○○○○○	10 A B C D E ○○○○○	17 A B C D E ○○○○○	24 A B C D E ○○○○○	31 A B C D E ○○○○○
4 A B C D E ○○○○○	11 A B C D E ○○○○○	18 A B C D E ○○○○○	25 A B C D E ○○○○○	32 A B C D E ○○○○○
5 A B C D E ○○○○○	12 A B C D E ○○○○○	19 A B C D E ○○○○○	26 A B C D E ○○○○○	33 A B C D E ○○○○○
6 A B C D E ○○○○○	13 A B C D E ○○○○○	20 A B C D E ○○○○○	27 A B C D E ○○○○○	34 A B C D E ○○○○○
7 A B C D E ○○○○○	14 A B C D E ○○○○○	21 A B C D E ○○○○○	28 A B C D E ○○○○○	35 A B C D E ○○○○○

BLANK PAGE

Selective High School Practice Test
Mathematical Reasoning 10 – Answer Sheet

Fill in the appropriate circle for your chosen answer

Eg.. A B C D E
○ ● ○ ○ ○

Use a pencil. If you make a mistake, erase thoroughly and try again.

NAME : **SCORE:**

1 A B C D E ○○○○○	8 A B C D E ○○○○○	15 A B C D E ○○○○○	22 A B C D E ○○○○○	29 A B C D E ○○○○○
2 A B C D E ○○○○○	9 A B C D E ○○○○○	16 A B C D E ○○○○○	23 A B C D E ○○○○○	30 A B C D E ○○○○○
3 A B C D E ○○○○○	10 A B C D E ○○○○○	17 A B C D E ○○○○○	24 A B C D E ○○○○○	31 A B C D E ○○○○○
4 A B C D E ○○○○○	11 A B C D E ○○○○○	18 A B C D E ○○○○○	25 A B C D E ○○○○○	32 A B C D E ○○○○○
5 A B C D E ○○○○○	12 A B C D E ○○○○○	19 A B C D E ○○○○○	26 A B C D E ○○○○○	33 A B C D E ○○○○○
6 A B C D E ○○○○○	13 A B C D E ○○○○○	20 A B C D E ○○○○○	27 A B C D E ○○○○○	34 A B C D E ○○○○○
7 A B C D E ○○○○○	14 A B C D E ○○○○○	21 A B C D E ○○○○○	28 A B C D E ○○○○○	35 A B C D E ○○○○○

BLANK PAGE

SELECTIVE PRACTICE TEST ANSWERS

Selective Practice Test Answers

Mathematical Reasoning 6

Question	Answer	Explanation
1	A	Option A is \$5/kg, option B is \$5.33/kg, option C is \$5.33/kg, option D is \$6/kg and option E is \$6/kg
2	C	25 000 + 1000 = 26 000.
3	D	Step 1 = 5cm Step 2 = 8cm Pattern: Step × 3 +2 = length If length is 158, Step=52
4	C	A => not included in specified range B => diff of 10.4 C => diff of 10.45 D => diff of 10.43 E => not included in specified range
5	E	The shaded area is 2/32 = **1/16**
6	A	Trial and error: When Mr Huang is **50** (42+8), John is 17+8 = 25, which is half of 50.
7	B	18/27 = 2/3. 2/3 * 360 = **240**
8	D	Mirrors reflect things along a vertical axis, meaning we flip it horizontally. The star will therefore, now be on the right side of his face.
9	B	(16 x 80 + 24 x 90)/(16 + 24) = 86%
10	B	There are 13 cubes left. 13 x 1000 = 13000

11	C	5=> 9=>17 using (2x-1) Thus total = 5+9+17 =31 students in total
12	C	1000000/25 = 40000
13	E	40 + 30 + 25 = 95
14	A	0.076 + 0.927 = 1.003
15	D	73 + 74 + 75 = 222. 222/3 = 74. Thus, the largest of these numbers is 75.
16	C	J+10=D, A+20=J, so A+30=D. Therefore, D+J+A= 3D-40=500, 3D= 540, so D=180. If D=180, =170 and A=150, so Andrew is 150 centimetres tall. Alternatively, test the answers, and you will find that C satisfies all the conditions given.
17	E	Use the answers to find out how much the younger child would have gotten if the older child had gotten that amount, then add both together to see if the result is $900
18	B	380/8 = 47.5 47.5 x 20 = **950**
19	C	The angles are all equal = 60 degrees; thus it is an **equilateral** triangle
20	A	X & Y have 50 students each, so 25 girls each, so 25 boys each. So X & Y combined have 50 boys. However, in Z, there is 100 members in total, of which a quarter are boys, so only 25 boys. In total, there are 75 boys.
21	B	Between 12 and 13 is a temperature difference of 13 degrees
22	C	(6 x (4 + 6)÷2) x 12 = 360
23	C	right hand side is a different colour such as green

24	A	$20 \times 3\frac{3}{4} = 75$
25	A	5 4 3 2 1 0 A B C D E F
26	E	1hr for 15 questions = 60 min for 15 questions = 4 min per question. For Maria to complete 5 questions = 5 x 4min = 20min Portia finished 5 questions 2 min before this but started 12 min earlier = 20-2 + 12 = 30min Therefore, she worked at 30min/5questions = 6 min per question Therefore, Portia took 6min x 15 = 90min = **1 hour 30 min**
27	A	From looking at the graph, the car was not travelling between 2 pm – 3 pm.
28	B	You can see from the graph that it is steepest between 1 pm – 2 pm, meaning this was when it was travelling the fastest.
29	B	The car trip lasts from 12 pm – 5 pm. In that span of 5 hours, 210km are travelled. 210 ÷ 5 = 42
30	E	5/20 = 1/4
31	D	Total cost of production: 25 dollars 100 x 25 x 50% x 20% = **250**
32	B	Number of papers Dennis has marked = (84-24)/2 = 30 Neil has marked 30+24 = 54 papers. Neil:Dennis = 54:30 = **9:5**
33	D	All the carrots combined is 1468. Therefore, the mass of all the apples is 1972-1468=504g. Then, each apple weighs 504÷2=252g

34	B	The total length of 24cm is composed of 3 times the radius length of one of the big circles. R = 24/3 = 8 cm Since the diameter of the shaded circle = 8 cm, radius = 4 $A = \pi r^2$ = 3.14 x 16 = **50.24 cm squared**
35	E	12.20x4 + 4.10x4 + 2x4 + 8.35x4 = 106.60

Selective Practice Test Answers

Mathematical Reasoning 7

Question	Answer	Explanation
1	A	31 788 will be rounded up to 32 000 (32 thousand) for the nearest thousand.
2	D	The triangle is isosceles as 2 sides are radii. Therefore, x = (180 -(130-50))/2 = **50**
3	C	33x25 = 825 825-360 = 465
4	B	Area = (10 x 15) – (4 x 4) - (5 x 7) = **99**
5	E	5 x 400 x 20/1000 = **40**
6	E	If ¼ play soccer, that means 225 students don't play soccer. Of those 225, 4/5 play T-ball, which means there are 45 play tennis
7	A	15 10 20 5 Mel Ann Jan Bel Fran The difference between first and fourth is 15 + 10 + 20 = 45m
8	C	Take any three-digit number as an example. E.g. 321 The number in the ten's place is 2. Increasing it by 1 gives the new number 331. This new number is 10 more than the old number.
9	A	Length = Step × 4 +1 Length = 10 × 4 +1 = 41
10	E	3*3.5 = 10.5 (if one sister does it) 10.5/5 = 2.1 (2hrs 6mins)

11	C	Ankita takes $\frac{1}{4}$ of the hair clips, so there are 90 left. Jessica takes $\frac{1}{2}$ of the remainder, so there are 45 left. If Andrew takes what's left, he takes 45
12	D	If the interest rate is 8%pa, then monthly it is 0.66%. If he invests his $4500 in for 3 months, he gets 2%, so 2% of $4500 is $90. As such, he has $4590 in the bank after 3 months
13	A	There is a difference of 5 - 2 = 3 parts. Therefore, the difference in heights must be a multiple of 3 (whole number heights). **24** is the only multiple of 3.
14	B	Total angle of the 2 together = 90 degrees Which is 25% of the graph. Tennis (67.5°)+ Volleyball (22.5°) $= 90°$
15	E	Total of Basketball and Cricket before was 3/8 Now add another ¼ (the total Soccer population is split between the two. New total = 5/8
16	B	J=S+4, J=T+8. Therefore, S=J-4, T=J-8. So J+T+S=3J-12=156, so J=56. And T=J-8=48. Alternatively, test the answers. If Terry is 48 kilograms, Sam is 52 kilogram and Jack is 56 kilograms, so their total mass is 156 kilograms
17	C	5% of 10 = 50c, thus 40/0.5 = 80, therefore **80** times.
18	A	Area of square = 8 × 8 = 64 cm^2 Area of triangle = 12 × 12 ÷ 2 = 72 cm^2 Difference = 72 – 64 = 8 cm^2
19	A	$42 - \frac{58}{2}$ =13. Total time = 13 + 13 = 26
20	C	10 small blocks 6x5x4x10 = 1200
21	A	Dennis invests 3500. Thornton invests 1400. Neil invests 2800. Raj invests 2000 3500 + 1400 + 2800 + 2000 = 9700 9700-5000 = 4700
22	C	There are 52 weeks in a year. The worker only works four days a week so in total, he works 208 days. 6240 divided by 208 = 30.

23	C	The numbers are 7 and 8. 7 + 8 = 15 (sum) 7 x 8 = 56 56 – 15 = 41 (as required).
24	E	Harry's length is $\frac{6}{5}$ of Ron's length, so Harry's is 42cm. Harry's length is $\frac{6}{7}$ of Hermoine's length, so Hermoine's is 49cm. The sum of their three wand's lengths is 35cm + 42cm + 49cm = 126cm
25	B	Find the number of children between the 5th and 12th child, this is 7. This is equal to half the circle, therefore the full circle would be 14 children
26	B	2 x 28 x 22/7 x 20 = 3520 cm = 35.2 m
27	D	multiple of 3 or 5 = {3, 6 , 9, 12, 15, 18, 5, 10, 20}.
28	D	★ = ■ ☺ ★ = ■ ■ ☼ ★ ☼ = ■ ■ ☼ ☼ = ☺ ☺
29	B	Lasith paid with 2 X 2 = $4 $4-$1.70 = $2.30 spent $2.30 – (2 x 0.25) – (3 x 0.30) = 0.90 spent on gummy bears 0.90/0.15 = 6.
30	C	The two triangles each take half of the rectangle, thus if separated and added, they take up the whole rectangle.
31	E	Paces = 1000/1.5 * 3 = **2000** paces
32	D	1000 x 40 = 40 000 cm^2 => 4 m^2 minimally, thus D

33	C	18.25+0.5=18.75 18.75+1-19.75 19.75+2=21.75 21.75+4=25.75 6th hour = 25.75 + 8 = 33.75 It will take 6 hours.
34	B	0.45 x 1000 = 450. HOWEVER, the answer requests centimetres. 10mm=1cm, therefore 450÷10=45cm
35	D	Use the key to the right of the picture to work it out. In diagram 4, his mother got 8 slices, his sister got 4 slices, his father got 6 slices and Raymond got 2 slices. This fits the information given.

Selective Practice Test Answers

Mathematical Reasoning 8

Question	Answer	Explanation
1	D	The largest possible number is 99 873. The smallest possible number is 37 899. The difference between these two is 99 873 – 37 899 = 61 974.
2	C	Find the pattern. The first diagram requires 3 matches, the second requires 9 and the third requires 18. The amount of extra matches from the first and second diagram is 6 and the number of extra matches from the second and third diagram is 9. Therefore we need 12 more matches to make the 4th diagram, which means we need 30 matches
3	C	40 minutes, 200 degrees. Therefore, the average per minute is 200÷40=5
4	E	Paid amount= $20-$6.40 = N+(12-N) x $1.2 ➔ N=4
5	B	1 – ¾ = ¼ . 1- 1/3 = 2/3. 1 – 2/3 = 1/3. Hence, ¼ x 2/3 = 1/6, and then 1/6 x 1/3 = 1/18
6	B	Kanye is the faster rapper. Work this out by finding out how many words per minute for each artist. Kanye = 117/13 * 60 = 540 Iggy = 164/41 * 60 = 240. Therefore, **Kanye wins by 300 words** in a minute.
7	B	F must be a 10 x 4 rectangle since its length = side of a square. Therefore, C must be a (10-4) x (10/5) = 6 by 2 rectangle = **12 cm²**
8	C	By mirroring the clock, the time says 1:40 am. If he woke up at 11am, therefore the time difference is 9 hours and 20 min.

9	E	4 boxes of noodles = 8 rolls of sushi. Therefore 13 rolls of sushi is 32.50 roll of sushi = 32.50/13 = \$2.50. Therefore a box of noodles is \$5.00 Hence 2 sushi rolls and a noodle box would cost \$10.
10	D	9/20 x N=63➔N=140, Therefore 1/5 x 3/28 x 140 = 3
11	A	Add a layer of blocks to each face and you now have a 5×7×5 shape
12	B	30 x 7 = 210 A: 14 x 15 = 210 **B: 20 x 11 = 220 is greater than 210 and requires the least number of working hours.** C: 19 x 13 = 247 D: 20 x 10 = 200 E: 17 x 12 = 204
13	E	The measuring wheel rotates 900° every minute, so it rotates 4050° in the 4.5 minutes. Now, 4050÷360=11.25, so the measuring wheel completes 11 full revolutions in that time
14	C	1 = 4cm 2 = 6cm 3 = 8cm ... ? = 100cm Pattern: number×2+2=length
15	D	500 = 40% 1% = 12.5 Total number of students = 1250 Drama = 5% Therefore 12.5 x 5 = 62.5 Which is closest to 62
16	C	Add 250 to 62 = 312

17	B	The combined age of the kids is 45. Sean is 59. Every year, the kids' combined age increases by 4 while Sean's age increases by 1. It takes 5 years for the kids' combined age to catch up.
18	E	B+S=16, B+M=19, M+S=11 ➔ B=12, M=7, S=4
19	D	0.95 * 700000 = 665 000.
20	C	Total picked by Eileen, Harry and Sarah = 44 Total picked by Bob and Timmy = 19 Difference between the two is 25
21	C	Average is 12.6 Bob is closest with 13
22	D	There are 150 students at the camp split in a ratio of 7:3. Divide 150 by 10 to give 15. Therefore, there are 105 boys and 45 girls. Therefore, there are 60 more boys than girls.
23	A	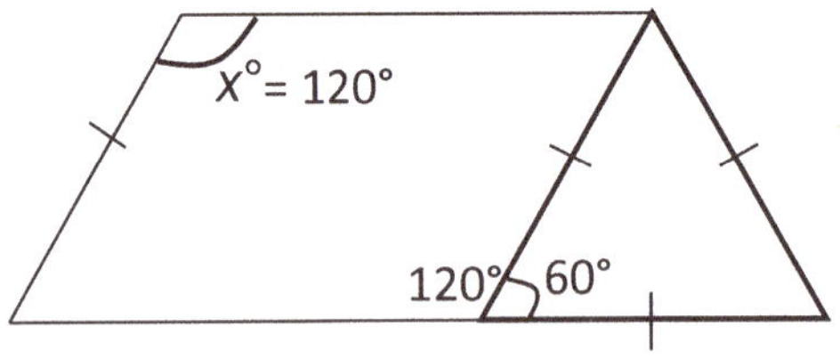 $x°$ = 120° 120° 60°
24	A	0.5 x 3.14 x 10 x 10 x 40 = 6280 mL = 6.28 L
25	E	John's marbles is 63/0.6 = 105, Paul's marbles is 105/(5/8) = 168
26	D	First find out the price of a pack of chips and the price of a chocolate bar using simultaneous equations. Then add them together
27	B	80-(4x4)=64
28	C	Same method as in 6, change the fractions into improper fractions and then the denominator into 40. $1\frac{1}{8}$ becomes 45/40 and $1\frac{2}{5}$. becomes 56/40. Hence there are 10 values for the numerator, ranging from 46-55
29	B	Total number of toys = 8N+15 = 10N-5 ➔ N=10

30	A	Add the first two equations: 2★ = 26 ★ = 13 Then ○ = 1 Substitute these into the last equation: ♣ = 8 ☆=2 Adding them all, the answer is 24.
31	B	Working with a half side of the 6x6 square, the number of 1x1 small squares = 4+2 plus two half squares. Total is 7.
32	C	Area of the 6×6 square is $36cm^2$, area of star is $14cm^2$, therefore $\frac{7}{18}$ is covered by star
33	B	50% have black eyes so 400 people have black eyes. 10% have green eyes, so 80 people have green eyes. The remaining amount of people is 320 people. Of the 320, 25% have blue eyes, so 80 have blue eyes. The remainder have brown eyes, so 240 people have brown eyes
34	E	Count backwards from Sunday to find out how many metres he runs each day. From Monday he runs 100m, increasing by 50m each day. Therefore, from Monday to Friday, he runs 100m + 150m + 200m + 250m+ 300m = 1000m.
35	E	4 x 6 x 3 = 72

Selective Practice Test Answers

Mathematical Reasoning 9

Question	Answer	Explanation
1	C	75000 + 669708 = 744708
2	D	South-West
3	C	Jar = 500g milk = 1500g
4	E	A: $3 \times 10^3 + 5 \times 10^3$ = 8 000 B: $5 \times 10^5 + 8 \times 10^6$ = 8 500 000 C: $6 \times 10^5 + 2 \times 10^5$ = 800 000 D: $20 \times 10^4 + 2 \times 10^3$ = 202 000 E: $4 \times 10^6 + 5 \times 10^6$ = 9 000 000
5	D	T = 70, H = 110, D = 90
6	B	[½ x 6 x (8 + 14) x 2] + [½ x 12 x 6 + ½ x 10 x 6] = 198
7	C	(6 x $0.30) + (12 x $0.60) = $9
8	B	$1 - \frac{1}{4} - \frac{1}{3} - \frac{1}{6} - \frac{1}{9} = \frac{36}{36} - \frac{9}{36} - \frac{12}{36} - \frac{6}{36} - \frac{4}{36} = \frac{5}{36}$ $\frac{5}{36}$ of the whole trucks = 5 black trucks Therefore, whole trucks = 36
9	B	A=4, B=5, C=6, D=7
10	B	One roll = 0.5m x 2m = $1m^2$ Therefore, 24 rolls = $24m^2$
11	D	$1.25 x 24 = $30
12	E	(3220-1000)/ 12 = $185

13	B	Read graph
14	C	Car 1 did not stop. Car 2 stopped for 1hr
15	D	Distance = 150km, Time = 2 hrs Speed = 150 / 2 = 75km/hr
16	E	Distance = 80km, Time = 2 hrs Speed = 80 / 2 = 40km/hr
17	B	1/5 = 75ml Full container = 375ml 2/3 = 250ml 250 – 150 = 100ml
18	C	★★★★☺☺ = ★★☺☺☺ ★★ = ☺ ★★☺☺ = 90g ★★★★★★ = 90g ★ = 15g
19	B	11,11
20	D	$\frac{3}{4}$ of 16 = 12 (won by more than 2 goals) 12 out of 24 = 50%
21	C	70% of Original value = \$3150 Original Value = \$3150 ÷ 0.7 Original Value = \$4500
22	E	350 - (52+66+70+75) = 87
23	B	Total Area in cm = 350cm x 50 cm = 17500cm^2 To find the number of tiles being used, 17500cm^2 ÷ (7cm x 25cm) = 100. 100 patterns = 400 tiles the ratio of black to white is 1:1. So, Jonathan needs 200 black tiles
24	A	\$9.5 x 40 box

25	B	27,28,29,30,31,32,33 (remove 30 stays the same)
26	A	4.5cm x 18 = 81cm
27	A	7.5 squares=> 9 + 1.5 + 0.75 units
28	C	10 x 8 = 80
29	B	450/10 = 45 45 x 7 = 315kg
30	E	5x2 = 10, now 10/3 = 3hr 20min then 5hr – 3hr 20min = 1hr 40min
31	A	♠ + ♠ + ♠ + ♣ = 26.5 ....(1) ♠ + ♠ + ♣ = 19.1 ....(2) (1) – (2) = ♠ = 7.4 7.4 + 7.4 + ♣ = 19.1 ♣ = 4.3
32	B	12 boys, 18 girls were original numbers
33	D	Volume of cylinder = πr^2 x h 3.14 x 25 x 10 = 785 cm^3
34	D	110 x 0.8 + 80 x 0.6 + 50 x 0.7 = **171**
35	E	The virus doubles itself every day, and takes 10 days to fill the petri dish. Therefore, 2**10=1024 to fill the petri dish. 16x 2**(?)=1024, So (?)=6

Selective Practice Test Answers

Mathematical Reasoning 10

Question	Answer	Explanation
1	C	For the average to be 6, we would need the total of the 6 numbers to be 6*6 = 36. Current sum = 33, therefore the number which was added was 3.
2	E	An even number squared added to another even number will always equal an even number.
3	C	92/7 = 13 remainder 1 Therefore the day of the week that Christmas will fall on is Tuesday.
4	B	The fraction is less than 8/11 = 64/88 The fraction is greater than 31/44 = 62/88 Therefore the numerator must be 63
5	A	(25 X $0.10) + (25 X $0.50) = $15
6	D	2(Zara + 5) = Indira + 5 Indira = Zara + 24 2Zara + 10 = Zara + 29 2Zara – Zara = 29 – 10 Zara = 19 Indira = 43
7	C	Together Luna and Celeste finish off 23/45 of a pizza. The remainder 22/45 is split between two people, so each person gets 11/45 of a pizza.
8	D	Each segment of a clock represents 1/12 of 360 degrees. This means each segment will equal 30 degrees. Between 8 and 12 there are 4 segments, and so the reflex angle will be 360 – (4*30) = 240 degrees
9	E	Calculate difference of starting and ending weight

10	C	You do not have any 5c coins and so $0.95 is not possible.
11	B	54/6 = 9 9*15 = 135
12	A	
13	C	17 = 1/5 of the pole Therefore, the pole is 85m in total. 110 – 85 = 25m
14	A	Going backwards – 290 – 271 = 19 19*12 = 228 228 + 6 = 234 The original number should have been 234 234 + 6 = 240 240/12 = 20 290 – 20 = 270
15	E	There should be 9 cubes with 3 faces painted.
16	E	(4-1) / 5 = 0.6 (each decrement) 4 -> 3.4 -> 2.8
17	B	If you cut all the corners off a hexagonal pyramid, you will have an additional 7 faces. There will now be a total of 14 faces. A dodecagonal prism also has 14 faces.
18	B	As the amount of builders is doubled but the amount of wall is also doubled,

19	E	Convert all prices into per kilo prices. 500g for \$2.10 = \$4.20/kg 1.5kg for \$4.85 = \$3.23/kg 750g for \$2.55 = \$3.40/kg 1.0kg for \$3.29 = \$3.29/kg 2.0kg for \$5.00 = \$2.50/kg Therefore the best value is E.
20	E	There are 153 students in Lucy's course. 153/7 = 21 r 6 153/8 = 19 r 1 There will be no students left over when dividing by 3.
21	B	B x h = 16 X 20 = 320m^2
22	D	Volume in cm^3 is 6×8×8=384cm^3
23	C	10% of the original borrowed amount is \$1000. Paying \$1000 for 4 years, he ends up paying back \$4000. However, this means he still has \$10000-\$4000 to pay which is \$6000
24	A	On Monday she eats 9kg, Tuesday 8.1kg, Wednesday 7.29kg, 73% of 10kg is 7.3kg which is closest to 7.29kg
25	A	Seth scored 4% of the goals. 1% of the goals = 16/4 = 4 Therefore Dylan scored 4*45 = 180
26	B	If Jake scored 51 goals and this is 17% of the goals, then 1% = 3 Sam would have scored 22*3 goals = 66
27	D	\$20000 x 4.4% = \$880 p.a. \$1760 for 2 years
28	B	36-28.26=7.74
29	C	X $\frac{1}{5}$ = 20% Y $\frac{1}{5}$ = 20% (only 5 out of all) Z $\frac{3}{5}$ = 60% (3,4,5 out of all)

30	C	3.6 KL = 3600L 5 L per 5 seconds = 1 L per second 4 L per 4 seconds = 1 L per second Total volume per second = 2L 3600/2 = 1800 seconds = 30 minutes
31	E	The coordinates will form a trapezium
32	D	6m - $\frac{2}{9}$m = 5 $\frac{7}{9}$m
33	A	10^4 = 10000 10000 + 50 = 10050 1 + 0 + 0 + 5 + 0 = 6
34	D	If Wallace is facing south, then turns 135 degrees anticlockwise, then he will be facing north east. Another 135 degrees anticlockwise is what he needs to turn in order to face west.
35	D	Per hour the total distance travelled between the two of them will be 7 km. 35km/7km = 5 hours